JANUA LINGUARUM

STUDIA MEMORIAE
NICOLAI VAN WIJK DEDICATA

edenda curat

C. H. VAN SCHOONEVELD

Indiana University

Series Minor, 192/1

FORMAL GRAMMARS IN LINGUISTICS AND PSYCHOLINGUISTICS

VOLUME I

An Introduction to the Theory of Formal Languages and Automata

by

W. J. M. LEVELT

1974

MOUTON

THE HAGUE · PARIS

Translation: Andrew Barnas

Printed in Belgium by N.I.C.I., Ghent

PREFACE

In the latter half of the 1950's, Noam Chomsky began to develop mathematical models for the description of natural languages. Two disciplines originated in his work and have grown to maturity. The first of these is the theory of formal grammars, a branch of mathematics which has proven to be of great interest to information and computer sciences. The second is generative, or more specifically, transformational linguistics. Although these disciplines are independent and develop each according to its own aims and criteria, they remain closely interwoven. Without access to the theory of formal languages, for example, the contemporary study of the foundations of linguistics would be unthinkable.

The collaboration of Chomsky and the psycholinguist, George Miller, around 1960 led to a considerable impact of transformational linguistics on the psychology of language. During a period of near feverish experimental activity, psycholinguists studied the various ways in which the new linguistic notions might be used in the development of models for language user and language acquisition. A good number of the original conceptions were naïve and could not withstand critical test, but in spite of this, transformational linguistics has greatly influenced modern psycholinguistics.

The theory of formal languages, transformational linguistics, psycholinguistics, and their mutual relationships are the theme of this work. Volume I is an introduction to the theory of formal languages and automata; grammars are treated only as formal systems, and no application of the theory, linguistic or other, is made. Volume II in turn deals with applications of those mathematical models to linguistic theory. Volume III treats applications of grammatical systems to models of language user and language learner, as well as the formal questions which have arisen as a result of such applications. The material is cumulative: Volume II supposes a general understanding of Volume I, and Volume III refers to the subjects dealt with in Volumes I and II. Volumes II and III have their own preface, so we can now turn to some introductory remarks with respect to the present volume.

Volume I, independent of the two following volumes, should be seen as an introduction to the theory of formal languages and automata. A number of similar introductions are available at the moment, but I have nevertheless undertaken the present work for three reasons. First, most available texts, because they suppose an acquaintance with sophisticated mathematical theories and methods, are beyond the reach of many students of linguistics and psychology. More often than not, Chomsky's and Miller's contributions to the *Handbook of Mathematical Psychology* prove too difficult for early graduate teaching. The present introduction is kept at a rather elementary level; a general knowledge of college mathematics will be sufficient to follow the text, although familiarity with the elements of set theory and statistics will certainly be an advantage.

Second, existing introductions treat a number of subjects which have little obvious relation to linguistics or psychology. The linguist or the psychologist is obliged to make his own selection from among a series of topics which he does not yet understand, and he might search in vain for a treatment of topics which are especially relevant to his field. Probabilistic grammars and grammatical inference, for example, are not treated in any of the existing introductions. Special attention has been paid to these topics in the present volume, but matters not directly relevant to linguistics or psychology have not been completely excluded, as a balanced presentation of the theory sets its own demands.

The third reason for writing this introduction is to supply readers of the two following volumes with a concise survey of the main notions of formal language theory used there. The subject index of this volume can be used to find definitions of technical terms: definitions are indicated by italicized page numbers.

Without the help and cooperation of many, these three volumes could not have been realized. A first version was written during a sabbatical year at The Institute for Advanced Study in Princeton, New Jersey. I am deeply grateful to Professor Duncan Luce and to The Institute for the invitation which made my stay possible. Much in this work is due to the help and insights of Professor George Miller, former director of the Harvard Center for Cognitive Studies, where the new psychology of language originated under his guidance. Thanks to him I was granted a Research Fellowship at the Center in 1965, and by happy coincidence, he too was at the Institute for Advanced Study when I was composing the text. His attentive advice was most useful, especially in the writing of the third volume. Likewise, regular discussions with Dr. Philip Johnson-Laird helped to clarify many of the psychological issues. Conversations with Professor Aravind Joshi on the subject matter of the first two volumes were also enormously stimulating and enjoyable; I profited almost daily from his erudition in the fields of both formal systems theory and mathematical linguistics.

Finally, I wish to express my gratitude to all those who have contributed by critically reading the text in the original Dutch version: Professor L. Verbeek, Dr. H. Brandt Corstius, Mr. R. Brons, Dr. G. Kempen, Dr. A. van der Ven, Mr. E. Schils, Mr. L. Noordman, Dr. A. De Wachter-Schaerlaekens, and Professor A. Kraak. Their remarks not only prevented the printing of many disturbing errors, but also led to many enriching additions to the text.

March 1973 *W. J. M. Levelt*
Nijmegen

TABLE OF CONTENTS

1

GRAMMARS AS FORMAL SYSTEMS

1.1. GRAMMARS, AUTOMATA, AND INFERENCE

The theory of formal languages originated in the study of natural languages. The description of a natural language is traditionally called a GRAMMAR; it should indicate how the sentences of a language are composed of elements, how elements form larger units, and how these units are related within the context of the sentence. The theory of formal languages proceeds from the need to provide a formal mathematical basis for such descriptions.

Chomsky, the founder of the theory, envisaged more than a simple refinement of traditional linguistic description. He was primarily concerned with a more thorough examination of the basis of linguistic theory. This involves such questions as "what are the goals of linguistic theory?", "what conditions must a grammar fulfill in order to be adequate in view of these goals?", and "what is the general form of a linguistic theory?" Without a formal basis, these and similar questions cannot be handled with sufficient precision. Volume II of this book will deal with these issues; it will be shown that a formal language can serve as a mathematical model for a natural language, while a formal grammar can act as a model for a linguistic theory.

From a mathematical point of view, grammars are FORMAL SYSTEMS, like Turing machines, computer programs, propositional logic, theories of inference, neural nets, and so forth. Formal systems characteristically transform a certain INPUT into a particular OUTPUT by means of completely explicit, mechanically applicable rules. Input and output are strings of symbols taken from a particular alphabet or VOCABULARY. For a formal grammar the input is an abstract START SYMBOL; the output is a string of "words" which constitutes a "sentence" of the formal "language". Therefore a grammar may be considered as a GENERATIVE system; this feature is often emphasized by the use of the term GENERATIVE GRAMMAR. The quotation marks around "word", "sentence", and "language" indicate that these terms are not used in their full linguistic sense, but rather are concepts which must be strictly defined within the formal system. In linguistic applications of formal language theory, as in Volume II of this book, care must be taken to establish the relationships between the formal and linguistic notions. In the present volume, however, we will no longer use the quotation marks, and will omit the adjective "formal" for both language and grammar where the context allows.

A second type of formal system can use the sentences of a language as input; its output is generally an abstract stop symbol. Systems of this type are called AUTOMATA, and may be considered as ACCEPTING SYSTEMS. The theory of automata is older than that of formal language, and historically it was rather surprising that the two theories showed such close parallels that they often appeared to be mere notational variants. One can very well use an automaton rather than a formal grammar as a model for a theory of natural language, but although this has in fact been done, the generative grammar remains the preferred model. The interchangeability of grammars and automata indicates that the distinction between generative and accepting is less fundamental than it may at first appear. It is primarily a conceptual distinction; there are indeed automata with no "preferential direction" such as Turing machines, and grammars which are accepting rather than generative systems such as categorical grammars. However, from the point of view of presentation and application, the dichotomy has its merits. In psycholinguistics in particular it has a natural interpretation with reference to SPEAKER-HEARER models. Volume III of this book will offer several examples of such applications.

The third and last type of formal system which will be discussed in this volume takes a sample of the sentences of a language as input; its output is a grammar which is in some way adequate for the language. Such systems are called GRAMMATICAL INFERENCE PROCEDURES. They can serve as models not only for linguistic discovery procedures (how can one find a grammar for a given corpus of sentences?) but also for theories of language acquisition.

The mathematical growth of formal language theory has resulted in an enormous extension of its range of applications. Beyond its obvious applications in the analysis of computer languages, the theory is used for the formal description of visual patterns (see Volume III, paragraph 3.6.7. for such picture grammars), for subdivisions of logic, and for several other fields which deal with the formal representation of knowledge.

Conversely, the integration of formal language theory into the theory of formal systems has made various mathematical tools, such as recursive function theory, available to the study of formal languages.

The reader, however, need not be acquainted with such areas of mathematics in order to understand the present work which is meant to be an introduction. Our discussion will be limited to the relationship between formal language theory on the one hand and the theories of automata and inference on the other. Each of these has rather direct linguistic and psycholinguistic applications, and it is precisely the possibility of application which has served as the principal, though not only, criterion for selecting properties of the theories for discussion. This does not alter the fact that it is better to treat the structure of grammar, of automata, and of inference from an abstract than from an applied point of view. Such is the method which we shall follow here, beginning with a formal definition of the concept "grammar".

1.2. THE DEFINITION OF "GRAMMAR"

For the formal definition of "grammar" we must introduce four concepts: terminal vocabulary, nonterminal vocabulary, production rule, and start symbol.

The TERMINAL VOCABULARY V_T is the set of terminal elements with which the sentences of a language may be constructed. Elements of V_T will be denoted by lower case letters from the beginning of the Latin alphabet. We write $a \in V_T$ or *a in* V_T when a belongs to the terminal vocabulary.

The NONTERMINAL VOCABULARY V_N consists of elements which are only used in the derivation of a sentence; they never occur as such in the sentences of the language. Elements of V_N are upper case Latin letters and are called VARIABLES or CATEGORY SYMBOLS.

V_N and V_T are disjoint: their intersection, $V_N \cap V_T$, is empty. Together V_N and V_T form the vocabulary V of the grammar, thus $V = V_N \cup V_T$. A string of elements in V, regardless of whether they are variables, terminal elements, or both, will be denoted by a lower case letter of the Greek alphabet. A string may have 0, 1, or more elements; the string of 0 elements is called the NULL-STRING, and is represented by λ. A string consisting exclusively of terminal elements may be denoted by a lower case letter from the end of the Latin alphabet.

The symbol V_T^* is used to denote the set of all finite strings of elements from the terminal vocabulary. For example, if V_T consists of two elements, a and b, i.e. $V_T = \{a, b\}$, V_T^* consists of λ, a, b, aa, ab, bb, ba, aaa, aab, aba, bba, ... If we wish explicitly to exclude the null-string λ, we write V_T^+, the set of all strings of positive length. Thus, $V_T^+ = V_T^* - \lambda$. Obviously, therefore, if V_T is not empty, then V_T^* and V_T^+ contain an infinite number of elements (strings). Analogously one can define V^* as the set of all possible strings of vocabulary elements, and V^+ as the set of all possible strings of vocabulary elements except the null-string. The length of a string α is denoted by $|\alpha|$; thus $|a| = 1$, $|aab| = 3$, and $|\lambda| = 0$.

The PRODUCTION RULES or productions of a grammar are ordered pairs of strings. They take the form $\alpha \to \beta$, where $\alpha \in V^+$ and $\beta \in V^*$. This means that string of elements α of positive length can be replaced by, or rewritten as, string of elements β, possibly λ. Such rules apply in any context, i.e. if α is part of a longer string $\gamma\alpha\delta$, then $\gamma\alpha\delta$ may be rewritten as $\gamma\beta\delta$ by the same rule. When a string is rewritten as another string by a single application of a production rule, we use the symbol $\Rightarrow$; thus $\gamma\alpha\delta \Rightarrow \gamma\beta\delta$. The latter string DERIVES DIRECTLY from the former. If there are productions such that $\alpha_1 \Rightarrow \alpha_2, \alpha_2 = \alpha_3, \ldots \alpha_{n-1} \Rightarrow \alpha_n$, we may write $\alpha_1 \stackrel{*}{\Rightarrow} \alpha_n$, read "$\alpha_1$ derives α_n". The set of productions of a grammar is denoted by P; the set may also be described as a CARTESIAN PRODUCT. The set of all possible rules consists of all ordered pairs of strings which can be constructed in this manner; it may be denoted by $V^+ \times V^*$, the cartesian product of V^+ and V^*. The productions of a grammar are a subset of this product: some strings of V^+ may be replaced by some strings in V^*. Thus $P \subset V^+ \times V^*$.

The START SYMBOL of a grammar is denoted by S (originally for "sentence"); it is a particular element of V_N.

We can at this point define a grammar as follows.

A GRAMMAR $G = (V_N, V_T, P, S)$ is a system consisting of a nonterminal vocabulary V_N, a terminal vocabulary V_T, a set of productions P, and a start symbol S, with the following properties:

(1) V_N, V_T and P are finite, nonempty sets.
(2) $V_N \cap V_T = 0$.
(3) $P \subset V^+ \times V^*$.
(4) $S \in V_N$.

A SENTENCE generated by G is every element s of V_T^* for which $S \stackrel{*}{\Rightarrow} s$, i.e. it is a terminal string derivable from S by the productions of P.

The LANGUAGE $L(G)$ generated by G is the set of sentences generated by G.

Two grammars G_1 and G_2 are (WEAKLY) EQUIVALENT if $L(G_1) = L(G_2)$, i.e. if they generate the same set of sentences. Another form of equivalence, STRONG EQUIVALENCE, will be discussed in Volume II, paragraph 2.1.

1.3. EXAMPLES

EXAMPLE 1.1. Let $G = (V_N, V_T, P, S)$, where $V_N = \{S\}$, i.e. S is the only nonterminal symbol, $V_T = \{a, b\}, P = \{S \to aS, S \to b\}$. Which language is generated by G? Repeated application of the first production gives $S \Rightarrow aS \Rightarrow aaS \Rightarrow aaaS$, etc. None of these strings is a sentence, for all include the nonterminal symbol S. The only way to eliminate S is by use of the second production $S \to b$. This will produce sentences such as b, ab, aab, $aaab$, etc. A sentence generated by G is thus a string of a's followed by a single b. A simple notation for language $L(G)$ is $\{a^*b\}$, where a^* is any string of a's of length $\geqslant 0$.

EXAMPLE 1.2. Let $G = (V_N, V_T, P, S)$, where $V_N = \{S\}$, $V_T = \{a, b\}$, $P = \{S \to aSa,\ S \to bSb,\ S \to aa,\ S \to bb\}$. The first two rules may be applied and repeated in any order. This will produce such derivations as $S \Rightarrow aSa \Rightarrow abSba \Rightarrow abbSbba \Rightarrow abbaSabba$. The only way to derive sentences from such strings is by use of the third or fourth production; these replace S with aa or bb. In all cases the result is a string of a's and b's, followed by the same string in reverse order. G is said to generate language $\{ww^R\}$, where w^R represents the reflection of w, and $|w| \geqslant 1$. $L(G)$ is called a MIRROR IMAGE language.

EXAMPLE 1.3. Let $G = (V_N, V_T, P, S)$, where $V_N = \{S,E,F\}$, $V_T = \{a, b, c, d\}$, $P = \{S \to ESF,\ S \to EF,\ E \to ab,\ F \to cd\}$. By applying the first production of P $n-1$ times, we obtain the string $E^{n-1}SF^{n-1}$ (the exponent indicates the number of successive occurrences of the element). By then using the second production once, one obtains E^nF^n. When, by application of the third and fourth productions respectively, all the E's are replaced by ab and all the F's by cd, the resulting string consists of n ab-pairs followed by n cd-pairs. Language $L(G)$ consists of all sentences of the form $(ab)^n(cd)^n$, where $n \geqslant 1$.

In this example a alternates with b, and c with d in the sentences of $L(G)$. It is possible to modify the grammar in such a way that the terminal elements will be neatly grouped in the sentences of L: first all a's, then all b's, etc. This will be the case in the following example.

EXAMPLE 1.4. Language $\{a^n b^n c^n d^n\}$, where $n \geqslant 1$, is generated by grammar $G = (V_N, V_T, P, S)$, in which $V_N = \{S, E, F, B, C\}$, $V_T = \{a, b, c, d\}$, and P consists of the following productions:

1. $S \rightarrow ESF$	4. $F \rightarrow Cd$	7. $BC \rightarrow bc$
2. $S \rightarrow EF$	5. $Ba \rightarrow aB$	8. $Bb \rightarrow bb$
3. $E \rightarrow aB$	6. $dC \rightarrow Cd$	9. $cC \rightarrow cc$

The first four productions are essentially the same as those of Example 1.3. They produce strings of the form $(aB)^n(Cd)^n$, where $n \geqslant 1$. The other five productions serve in the further grouping of the elements. By means of production 5 one can replace a string $aBaBaB...$ of arbitrary length by a string of a's followed by a string of B's. Production 6 acts similarly with respect to $CdCdCd...$ sequences. We must now see to it that further rewriting in terminal symbols is possible only when these arrangements have in fact been performed; this is the purpose of rules 7 through 9. Rule 7 serves to replace the pair BC in the center of the string with terminal elements, but it can be applied only if B and C are found in the right place in the center of the string. By means of production 8 the variables B are replaced by the terminal symbol b, on condition that each B is located directly to the left of a b. The process can be completed only when all the B's are already in the correct positions. Finally production 9 acts similarly in the right hand half of the string. The result is a string of the desired form, $a^n b^n c^n d^n$; sentences of other forms cannot be generated by this grammar.

EXAMPLE 1.5. It is possible to write a still more compact grammar for language $\{a^n b^n c^n d^n\}$, namely $G = (V_N, V_T, P, S)$, in which $V_N = \{S, E, F\}$, $V_T = \{a, b, c, d\}$, and P consists of the following productions:

1. $S \rightarrow ESF$	4. $dF \rightarrow Fd$
2. $S \rightarrow abcd$	5. $Eb \rightarrow abb$
3. $Ea \rightarrow aE$	6. $cF \rightarrow ccd$

The reader himself may now experiment with the operation of this grammar.

2

THE HIERARCHY OF GRAMMARS

2.1. CLASSES OF GRAMMARS

The definition of grammar given in the preceding chapter is absolutely general in the following intuitive sense: if a mechanical procedure can be contrived, according to which the sentences of language *L* can be enumerated in some order, then language *L* can be generated by a grammar in the defined form. We call this statement intuitive because the concept "mechanical procedure" has not yet been defined. One definition of it will be given in paragraph 7.4., but for the present one can roughly conceive of it as follows. Let us assume that we dispose of a general purpose computer with an unlimited memory. Let us further assume that a program can be written for this computer according to which each sentence of *L*, and only sentences of *L*, will appear in the output after a finite number of operations. (The program might, for example, produce the sentences in order of length: first λ if it is in the language, then the sentences of length 1, followed by the sentences of length 2, etc.) We could then say that a procedure exists for the enumeration of the sentences of *L*, and that *L* is RECURSIVELY ENUMERABLE. Every recursively enumerable language can be generated by a grammar corresponding to the definition (we shall return to this matter in paragraph 7.4.).

The class of recursively enumerable languages is large, but it is of little interest from a linguistic point of view. One would expect that natural languages have characteristic properties which would rather limit the range of possible syntactic structures in certain respects. The class of recursively enumerable languages is therefore an unattractive model for natural languages because it is defined by procedures which may be completely arbitrary. Models of empirical interest will result only from the definition of more limited classes of grammars. It is better to reject too strong a model with good reason than to maintain a weak model and never discover the characteristic structure of a language. The class of recursively enumerable languages is the weakest conceivable model.

Chomsky (1959 a, b) devised a schema for the classification of grammars which is now in general use. It is based on three increasingly restrictive conditions on the production rules.

FIRST LIMITING CONDITION: For every production $\alpha \rightarrow \beta$ in P, $|\alpha| \leqslant |\beta|$. Thus the grammar contains no productions whose application would result in a decrease of string length.

SECOND LIMITING CONDITION: For every production $\alpha \rightarrow \beta$ in P, (1) α consists of only one variable, i.e. $\alpha \in V_N$, and (2) $\beta \neq \lambda$. The productions are of the form $A \rightarrow \beta$, where $\beta \in V^+$.

THIRD LIMITING CONDITION: For every production $\alpha \rightarrow \beta$ in P, (1) $\alpha \in V_N$, and (2) β has the form a or aB, where $a \in V_T$ and $B \in V_N$. The rules are thus either of the form $A \rightarrow a$ or of the form $A \rightarrow aB$.

With these limiting conditions, grammars may be classified in the following way.

TYPE-0 GRAMMARS are grammars which are not restricted by any of the limiting conditions. Their definition is simply that of "grammar"; they are also called UNRESTRICTED REWRITING SYSTEMS. Productions are of the form $\alpha \rightarrow \beta$.

TYPE-1 GRAMMARS are grammars restricted by the first limiting condition. Productions have the form $\alpha \rightarrow \beta$, where $|\alpha| \leqslant |\beta|$. Type-1 grammars are also called CONTEXT-SENSITIVE GRAMMARS for reasons to be mentioned in paragraph 2.4. They obviously constitute a subclass of type-0 grammars. In fact they are a strict subset of the set of type-0 grammars, for there are type-0 grammars which are not of type-1, namely, those grammars with at least one production where $|\alpha| > |\beta|$. The grammars given in Examples 1.1. through 1.5. satisfy this first condition and are therefore context-sensitive.

TYPE-2 GRAMMARS are grammars restricted by the second limiting condition. Productions have the form $A \rightarrow \beta$ where $\beta \neq \lambda$. Grammars of this type are called CONTEXT-FREE GRAMMARS. The second condition implies the first: from $|\beta| \geqslant 1$ and $|A| = 1$ it follows that $|A| \leqslant |\beta|$. Context-free grammars are therefore context-sensitive, but the inverse is not true; the class of context-free grammars is a strict subset of the class of context-sensitive grammars. The grammars given in Examples 1.1., 1.2., and 1.3. are context-free.

TYPE-3 GRAMMARS are grammars restricted by the third limiting condition. Productions have the form $A \rightarrow a$ or $A \rightarrow aB$. These are REGULAR GRAMMARS (in linguistic literature they are often called FINITE STATE GRAMMARS). In its turn the third limiting condition implies the second. Therefore the class of regular grammars is a subclass of the class of context-free grammars; in fact it is a strict subset. The grammar given in Example 1.1. is a regular grammar.

Language types may be defined according to the various classes of grammars. A type-3 grammar generates a regular language (or finite state language), a type-2 grammar generates a context-free language, a type-1 grammar generates a context-sensitive language, and a type-0 grammar generates a (recursively enumerable) language.

It does not follow, however, from the relations of inclusion which exist among the various types of grammars that corresponding languages are bound by the same relations of inclusion. We cannot exclude the possibility a priori that for every context-free grammar there might exist an equivalent regular grammar. In that case all context-free languages might be generated by regular grammars, and consequently regular languages would not form a strict subset of context-free grammars. However in the following it will become apparent that the language types do show the same relations of strict inclusion as the grammar types: there are type-0 languages which are not context-sensitive, context-sensitive languages which are not context-free, and context-free languages which are not regular. Figure 2.1. illustrates this hierarchical relation, called the Chomsky Hierarchy.

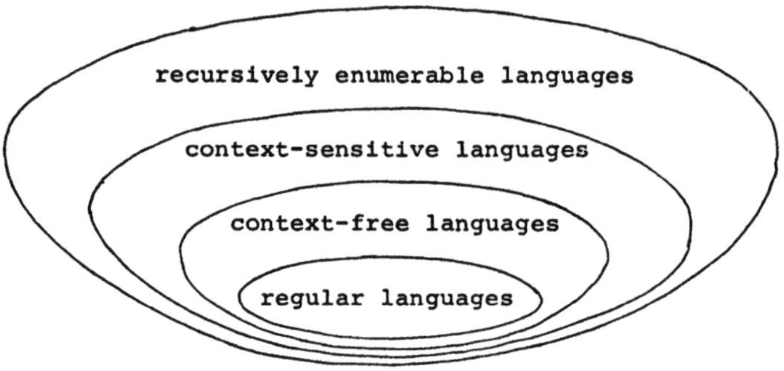

Fig. 2.1. The Chomsky Hierarchy of Languages.

It is obvious that the null-string can be present only in type-0 languages. Sometimes, however, it is convenient to add it to other languages as well. In the following we shall suppose in all cases, except in Chapter 3, that λ has been added to the language, unless otherwise stated.

In the remaining part of this chapter we shall deal with a few properties of each of the grammars.

2.2. REGULAR GRAMMARS

Most properties of regular grammars (*RG*'s) can best be treated on the basis of the theory of automata (cf. chapter 4). Our discussion here will be limited to five theorems which will be needed in the remainder of the present chapter; four of them can easily be explained without reference to automata theory.

We must first introduce a means of visual representation of grammatical derivations, called DERIVATION TREES, TREE DIAGRAMS, or PHRASE MARKERS (*P*-markers). The procedure is a general one which may be used not only for regular grammars, but also for context-free grammars and some context-sensitive grammars. An example will illustrate the procedure.

EXAMPLE 2.1. Let $G = (V_N, V_T, P, S)$, where $V_N = \{S,B\}$, $V_T = \{a, b\}$, and $P = \{S \rightarrow aB,\ B \rightarrow bS,\ B \rightarrow b\}$. G is thus a regular grammar. The sentences in $L(G)$ consist of alternating a's and b's, beginning with a and ending with b. Thus $L(G) = \{(ab)^*\}$ (by convention $\lambda \in L(G)$).

Let us examine the derivation of the sentence *ababab*; it can be generated only in the following way: $S \Rightarrow aB \Rightarrow abS \Rightarrow abaB \Rightarrow ababS \Rightarrow ababaB \Rightarrow ababab$. Figure 2.2.a. gives the tree diagram for this derivation, clearly illustrating each step. Beginning at S (at the top of the diagram), the tree divides into two branches, one leading to a, the other to B; this is the first step in the derivation. From B two further branches lead to b and to S respectively, showing the second step. The remaining steps in the derivation may be discovered by inspection.

Formally speaking, a (derivation) tree is a system of nodes and branches (or edges). Branches are directed connections between nodes, i.e. branches enter and leave the nodes. A tree has only one node which no branch enters; it is called the root or origin of the tree. Exactly one branch enters each of the remaining nodes. Moreover, a path may be found from each node to the root of the tree. Finally, each node bears a label.

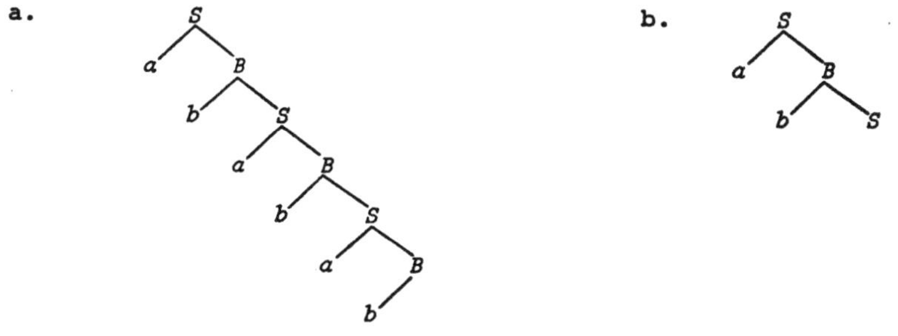

Fig. 2.2. a. Derivation Tree for the Sentence *ababab* (Example 2.1.).
b. Incomplete Derivation Tree.

A derivation in a context-free grammar can be represented by a tree diagram, all the nodes of which are labeled with elements of V. The root is the start symbol S, nodes from which branches leave are elements of V_N, and nodes from which no branches leave are elements of V_T. Each of these features can easily be verified in Figure 2.2.a.

Sometimes it is considered unnecessary to show the entire derivation, and only the first few steps are given in an incomplete tree, as in Figure 2.2.b. In such a case it is possible that nodes from which no branches leave may be labeled as elements of V_N.

We can now return to the subject of regular grammars. It is evident that each string in a regular grammar derivation contains at most one variable, and that this variable is the last element of the string. Consequently, tree diagrams for such derivations branch to the right, i.e. at each step it is the rightmost node which further divides into two branches.

The definition given for regular grammars is in some sense economical. It is possible that the class of languages generated by regular grammars be generated also by grammars with a more complicated rule structure. While this fact is not interesting in itself, it should caution us against concluding on the class to which a language might belong solely on the basis of the type of grammar by which it is generated. An example will serve to illustrate this.

EXAMPLE 2.2. Let $G = (V_N, V_T, P, S)$, with $V_N = \{S\}$, $V_T = \{a\}$, and $P = \{S \to aSa, S \to aa, S \to a\}$. This is obviously a context-free grammar; the productions are not of the form of those of regular grammars. But $L(G)$ is a regular language, for there is also a regular grammar by which it can be generated. $L(G)$ consists of all possible strings of a's; it can likewise be generated by grammar G' with $P' = \{S \to aS, S \to a\}$. G' is thus a regular grammar equivalent to G, and consequently $L(G)$ is a regular language.

A grammar is called RIGHT-LINEAR if all its productions are of the form $A \to xB$ or $A \to x$ (notice that x represents a string of terminal elements).

THEOREM 2.1. The class of right-linear grammars generates precisely the class of regular languages.

PROOF. All regular grammars are right-linear, and therefore all regular languages can be generated by right-linear grammars. The inverse, that each right-linear grammar has an equivalent regular grammar, must also be shown to be true. Let $G = (V_N, V_T, P, S)$ be a right-linear grammar. We must show that there is a regular grammar G' such that $L(G') = L(G)$. Take $G' = (V'_N, V'_T, P', S)$ with the following composition. For every production $A \to x$ in P, where $x = a_1a_2 \ldots a_n$, P' contains the following set of productions: $A \to a_1A_1$, $A_1 \to a_2A_2$, ..., $A_{n-2} \to a_{n-1}A_{n-1}$ and $A_{n-1} \to a_n$. These productions are clearly of the prescribed regular form, and A generates x. If we see to it that the variables $A_1, A_2, \ldots, A_{n-1}$ do not occur in any other production of P', G' will generate *only* x. Likewise for each production of the type $A \to xB$ in P, where $x = b_1b_2 \ldots b_m$, let P' contain a set of productions $A \to b_1B_1$, $B_1 \to b_2B_2$, ..., $B_{m-1} \to b_mB$, also taking care that the new variables $B_1, B_2, \ldots, B_{m-1}$ appear only in these productions. Further, let the nonterminal vocabulary V'_N contain V_N plus all the new variables introduced in the above way, and $V'_T = V_T$. It follows from the construction that $L(G') = L(G)$.

THEOREM 2.2. A context-free grammar, with productions such that all derivations are either of the form xB or of the form x, generates a regular language. The same holds if all derivations are of the form Bx or x.

PROOF (summarized). If all the derivations of a context-free grammar must be of the form xB or x, then all the productions must have the form $A \to xB$ or $A \to x$. It follows from Theorem 2.1. that such grammars only generate regular languages. A similar argument holds for grammars, all the derivations of which have the form Bx or x, but it must be shown that grammars with productions exclusively of the form $A \to Ba$ or $A \to a$ generate only regular languages.

THEOREM 2.3. All finite languages are regular.

PROOF. Let L be the finite set $\{s_1, s_2, ..., s_n\}$, where $s_i = a_{i1}a_{i2} ... a_{ih_i}$. One can generate s_i by a finite set of regular productions, namely $S \to a_{i1}A_{i1}$, $A_{i1} \to a_{i2}A_{i2}$, ..., $A_{ih_i-1} \to a_{ih_i}$, following the construction used in the proof of Theorem 2.1. The combination of all sets of productions for all s_i gives a finite regular grammar which generates L.

THEOREM 2.4. The union of two regular languages is regular.

PROOF. Let L_1 and L_2 be regular languages. We must show that L_3, where $L_3 = L_1 \cup L_2$ (i.e. L_3 consists of all the sentences of L_1 and all the sentences of L_2), is also regular. Let $G_1 = (V_N^1, V_T^1, P^1, S^1)$ be a regular grammar which generates L_1, and $G_2 = (V_N^2, V_T^2, P^2, S^2)$ be a regular grammar which generates L_2, taking care that $V_N^1 \cap V_N^2 = \emptyset$ (this is always possible). We compose grammar $G_3 = (V_N^3, V_T^3, P^3, S)$ as follows. (1) $V_N^3 = V_N^1 \cup V_N^2 \cup S$, i.e. V_N^2 contains the variables of G_1 and G_2 plus a new variable S, which will also serve as the start symbol of G_3. (2) $V_T^3 = V_T^1 \cup V_T^2$. (3) P^3 contains all productions P^1 and P^2 as well as all possible productions $S \to \alpha$ such that either $S^1 \to \alpha$ is a production in P^1, or $S^2 \to \alpha$ is a production in P^2. Thus $S \Rightarrow \alpha$ in G_3 in precisely the cases where $S^1 \Rightarrow \alpha$ in G_1 and $S^2 \Rightarrow \alpha$ in G_2. Therefore $L_3 = L_1 \cup L_2$. Because all the productions of G_3 are of the required regular form, L_3 is regular.

L_3 may be called the PRODUCT of L_1 and L_2 if L_3 consists of all strings xy with x in L_1 and y in L_2.

THEOREM 2.5. The product of two regular languages is regular. (This theorem will be proven in paragraph 4.4. in connection with the discussion of finite automata.)

2.3. CONTEXT-FREE GRAMMARS

The definition of context-free grammars (*CFG*) is less economical than that of regular grammars. Any production of the form

$A \to \beta$, where $|\beta| \neq 0$, is allowed; β can therefore be any string of terminal and nonterminal elements. However, one can greatly simplify the form of productions without diminishing the generative capacity of the grammars. Such simplified forms of grammars are called NORMAL-FORMS. The most important normal-forms of context-free grammars are the CHOMSKY NORMAL-FORM and the GREIBACH NORMAL-FORM. We shall discuss each of these, and will likewise prove that every context-free grammar is equivalent to a grammar of the Chomsky normal-form.

2.3.1. *The Chomsky Normal-Form*

A grammar is said to be of the Chomsky normal-form if all productions have the form $A \to BC$ or $A \to a$.

THEOREM 2.6. Any context-free language can be generated by a grammar of the Chomsky normal-form.

PROOF. By definition a context-free language can be generated by a grammar with productions of the form $A \to \beta$. We can distinguish three possibilities for such productions: (1) $\beta \in V_T$ (2) $\beta \in V_N$, (3) all other cases. In order to construct a grammar G' in Chomsky normal-form and equivalent to context-free grammar G, we must see if production forms (1), (2), and (3) can be replaced by the appropriate normal production forms. (1) Productions $A \to \beta$, where $\beta = a$, are of the required form and call for no further discussion. (2) If $A \to B$ is a production of G, there are two possibilities: (a) G contains no productions of the form $B \to x$, i.e. B cannot be further rewritten; in this case we can simply ignore the production $A \to B$ in the construction of G'. (b) B can be further rewritten in G, for instance by the productions $B \to \beta_1$, $B \to \beta_2, \ldots, B \to \beta_n$. Without diminishing the generative capacity of the grammar we can now replace these productions, as well as $A \to B$ with the set of productions $A \to \beta_1$, $A \to \beta_2, \ldots, A \to \beta_n$. In spite of rewriting, one or more of these new productions may retain the same form, for instance $A \to C$. In that case we can repeat the procedure and replace $A \to C$ by the productions $A \to \gamma_i$

for every γ_i for which $C \rightarrow \gamma_i$. This can in its turn lead to the same problem, but, as G contains a finite number of variables, the process will reach an end, except if the replacement chain contains a loop (for example $A \rightarrow B$, $B \rightarrow C$, $C \rightarrow A$). But in that case, the variables in the loop are interchangeable, and one of them, A for instance, can replace the others in all the productions of the grammar. The result is that all the newly constructed productions are of form (1) or (3). Those of form (1) are of the Chomsky normal-form. Both the new productions of form (3) and the original form (3) productions from G can be treated as follows.
(3) In the remaining productions $A \rightarrow \beta$, β consists of terminal and/or nonterminal elements. We replace all the terminal elements with new variables. Assume that the ith element of β is a terminal element b_i; we replace it with a new variable B_i, and add the production $B_i \rightarrow b_i$, which is of the required normal form. By repeating the operation for all terminal elements in β, we replace the production $A \rightarrow \beta$ by a production $A \rightarrow B_1B_2 \ldots B_n$ and a terminal production of the form mentioned above. Finally we must replace nonterminal productions with productions of the form $A \rightarrow BC$. Here we again apply the construction used in the proof of theorem 2.1., replacing production $A \rightarrow B_1B_2 \ldots B_n$ with a set of productions $A \rightarrow B_1D_1$, $D_1 \rightarrow B_2D_2$, ... $D_{n-2} \rightarrow B_{n-1}B_n$, which are all of the required form. It follows from the construction that grammar G' thus obtained is equivalent to G and in the Chomsky normal-form.

EXAMPLE 2.3. Let $G = (V_N, V_T, P, S)$, where $V_N = \{S,A,B\}$, $V_T = \{a,b\}$, and P contains the following productions:

1. $S \rightarrow aSB$	3. $A \rightarrow ab$
2. $S \rightarrow A$	4. $B \rightarrow b$

G generates all strings of the form a^nb^n ($n \geqslant 1$ when λ is excluded). Sentence a^3b^3, for example, has the following derivation: $S \Rightarrow aSB \Rightarrow aaSBB \Rightarrow aaSBb \Rightarrow aaSbb \Rightarrow aaabbb$. We shall now construct a grammar G' in the Chomsky normal-form and equivalent to G.

The only production in the required form is production 4; all others must be replaced. Beginning with production 1, we replace $S \to aSB$ with two productions $S \to CSB$ and $C \to a$, as in (2) in the above proof. $S \to CSB$ can in turn be replaced by $S \to CD$ and $D \to SB$, as in (1).

In production 2 we first replace A with the strings as which it can be directly rewritten. In the present case, the only such string is ab (cf. production 3), and production 2 is thus replaced by $A \to ab$. The normal-form can be obtained by the replacement of a and b with new variables and the addition of two terminal productions. As we already dispose of terminal productions $C \to a$ (from production 1) and $B \to b$ (production 4), it is sufficient to replace production 2 with $S \to CB$. Production 3 is at the same time replaced by productions of the required form. Thus G' contains the following productions:

1. $S \to CB$	3. $S \to CD$
2. $D \to SB$	4. $C \to a$
	5. $B \to b$

The derivation of sentence a^3b^3 in G' is therefore $S \Rightarrow CD \Rightarrow aD \Rightarrow aSB \Rightarrow aCDb \Rightarrow aaDb \Rightarrow aaSBb \Rightarrow aaSbb \Rightarrow aaabbb$.

Although grammars G and G' are equivalent, the derivations differ. This can easily be observed from the derivation trees for sentence a^3b^3 given in Figure 2.3.a. (derivation in G) and Figure 2.3.b. (derivation in G').

2.3.2. *The Greibach Normal-Form*

A grammar is in the Greibach normal-form if all the productions are of the form $A \to a\beta$, where β is a string of 0 or more variables ($\beta \in V_N^*$).

THEOREM 2.7. Any context-free language can be generated by a grammar in the Greibach normal-form.

For the proof of this theorem we refer the reader to Greibach (1965). Our discussion here will be limited to the following example.

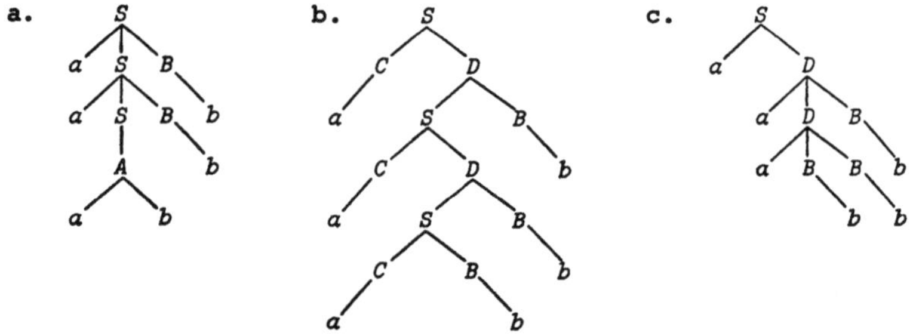

Fig. 2.3. Derivation Trees for a^3b^3.
a. Derivation Tree in G.
b. Derivation Tree in G' (Chomsky normal-form).
c. Derivation Tree in G'' (Greibach normal-form).

EXAMPLE 2.4. Let us once again consider grammar G of Example 2.3. In order to find a grammar G'' in Greibach normal-form which is equivalent to it, we may use grammar G' in Chomsky normal-form as starting point. The variables of G' are S, B, C, and D. We number these in an arbitrary order, indicating the number by subscript: thus, S_1, B_2, C_3, D_4. We shall at this point change the productions in such a way that the direct rewriting of a variable has as its first element either a terminal element or a variable with a higher number. Production 1 ($S_1 \rightarrow C_3B_4$) and production 3 ($S_1 \rightarrow C_2D_4$) already have this form. Production 2 ($D_4 \rightarrow S_1B_2$) can be adapted by first replacing S_1 with the strings as which it can be directly rewritten, namely C_3B_2 and C_3D_4, giving $D_4 \rightarrow C_3B_2B_2$ and $D_4 \rightarrow C_3D_4B_2$. It remains the case that the subscripts decrease (from 4 to 3), but the required form can be obtained by replacing C_3 in both productions with the only string as which it can be rewritten, a (see production 4). This gives the productions $D_4 \rightarrow aB_2B_2$ and $D_4 \rightarrow aD_4B_2$. Productions 4 ($C \rightarrow a$) and 5 ($B \rightarrow b$) are already of the required form. Recapitulating, at this point we have the following productions: $S_1 \rightarrow C_3B_2$, $S_1 \rightarrow C_3D_4$, $D_4 \rightarrow aD_4B_2$, $D_4 \rightarrow aB_2B_2$, $C_3 \rightarrow a$, $B_2 \rightarrow b$.[1]

[1] This example is relatively simple, as the case where the two subscripts are equal does not occur. In that case a special procedure is applied, and it is this which is the heart of Greibach's proof. We refer the reader to her original article, or to Hopcroft and Ullman (1969).

The first two productions are not yet of the Greibach normal-form; we thus replace the variable C_3 in these two productions with the only string as which it can be rewritten, a, thus also eliminating the need for the production $C_3 \rightarrow a$. In this way we arrive at the following productions for grammar G'' in Greibach normal-form (the subscripts are no longer necessary):

1. $S \rightarrow aB$
2. $S \rightarrow aD$
3. $D \rightarrow aBB$
4. $D \rightarrow aDB$
5. $B \rightarrow b$

Grammar G'' will thus generate sentence a^3b^3 as follows: $S \Rightarrow aD \Rightarrow aaDB \Rightarrow aaaBBB \Rightarrow aaaBBb \Rightarrow aaaBbb \Rightarrow aaabbb$. The tree diagram for this derivation is given in Figure 2.3.c.

2.3.3. *Self-embedding*

The economical production forms for context-free languages, especially the Chomsky normal-form ($A \rightarrow a$, $A \rightarrow BC$), show the minute difference in type of production which distinguishes context-free and regular languages (the regular form is $A \rightarrow a$ or $A \rightarrow bC$). What is the characteristic difference between these two classes of languages? One important property characterizing all nonregular context-free languages and absent in regular languages is that of SELF-EMBEDDING.

A context-free grammar $G = (V_N, V_T, P, S)$ is called self-embedding if there is a variable B in V_N, and elements α and γ in V^+ such that $B \overset{*}{\Rightarrow} \alpha B \gamma$.

Thus there is a variable B which, by application of the productions, can be rewritten as a string in which B itself occurs, but neither at the beginning nor at the end. The definition implies that a regular grammar is not self-embedding, since nonterminal symbols occur in regular derivations only at the end of a string.

A language is self-embedding if all grammars generating it are self-embedding.

It is therefore not sufficient that one of its grammars be self-embedding, as some self-embedding grammars merely generate regular languages. This is the case with the grammar of Example 2.2. Its productions are $S \to aSa$ $S \to aa$, $S \to a$, generating the language $\{a^n | n \geqslant 1\}$. The language is regular, but the grammar is self-embedding because $S \Rightarrow aSa$. The same example showed that G', with productions $S \to aS$ and $S \to a$, generates the same language. Grammar G' is not self-embedding, and generates $L(G)$, and consequently, by definition, $L(G)$ is not self-embedding.

THEOREM 2.8. All nonregular context-free languages are self-embedding, and all self-embedding languages are nonregular.

PROOF. The second member of this theorem follows directly from the definitions. A self-embedding language is generated exclusively by self-embedding grammars; a self-embedding grammar is, as we have seen, nonregular. Therefore a self-embedding language is nonregular.

The first member of the theorem can be otherwise formulated. It must be shown that all grammars of a nonregular context-free language are self-embedding. This can be done by proving that if a language L is generated by a non-self-embedding grammar, it is necessarily a regular language. To do this, however, we shall have to refer to a lemma which in turn will be easy to prove after the discussion of finite automata in Chapter 4.

Lemma. Let L_1 and L_2 be regular languages, and a be a terminal element of L_1. Let L_3 be a language consisting of all sentences in L_1 in which the element a does not occur, as well as all strings which can be obtained by replacing the element a in the remaining sentences of L_1 with a sentence of L_2 (if L_2 is infinite, this can be done in an infinite number of ways). L_3 is then a regular language.

We shall now prove that a language generated by a grammar which is not self-embedding is a regular language. Let language L be generated by a grammar G which is not self-embedding and which contains the variables $A_1, A_2, \ldots, A_n$.

Let us assume that grammar G is connected: a grammar is CONNECTED if for each pair of variables A_i, A_j $(i,i = 1, 2, \ldots, \text{n}$, where n is the number of variables in the grammar), there are strings α_1 and α_2 in V^* such that $A_i \overset{*}{\Rightarrow} \alpha_1 A_j \alpha_2$. Let A_i, A_j be an arbitrary pair of variables in G. Since G is connected, we have $A_i \overset{*}{\Rightarrow} \varphi_1 A_j \varphi_2$ for some pair φ_1, φ_2. Let us further assume that $|\varphi_1| > 0$. Let A_k, A_l also be an arbitrary pair of variables in G, with $A_k \overset{*}{\Rightarrow} \psi_1 A_l \psi_2$, and assume that $|\psi_2| > 0$. Let us examine the consequences of the two conditions $|\varphi_1| > 0$ and $|\psi_2| > 0$. It follows from the fact that G is connected that strings ω_1 and ω_2 exist such that $A_j \overset{*}{\Rightarrow} \omega_1 A_k \omega_2$ and that one can therefore make the following derivation in G: $A_i \overset{*}{\Rightarrow} \varphi_1 A_j \varphi_2 \overset{*}{\Rightarrow} \varphi_1 \omega_1 A_k \omega_2 \varphi_2 \overset{*}{\Rightarrow} \varphi_1 \omega_1 \psi_1 A_l \psi_2 \omega_2 \varphi_2$. But it follows from the same fact that $A_l \overset{*}{\Rightarrow} \xi_1 A_i \xi_2$. Therefore we have the following derivation in G: $A_i \overset{*}{\Rightarrow} \varphi_1 \omega_1 \psi_1 \xi_1 A_i \xi_2 \psi_2 \omega_2 \varphi_2$. It follows from the two additional conditions that A_i is self-embedding in G. But G is not self-embedding. At least one of the additional conditions must not be valid for a grammar to be connected, i.e. if a connected grammar has a pair of variables A_i, A_j, for which $A_i \overset{*}{\Rightarrow} \alpha_1 A_j \alpha_2$ with $|\alpha_1| > 0$, then there is no pair of variables for which $|\alpha_2| > 0$, including the pair A_i, A_j. Therefore all the derivations in G are either all of the forms xA and x, or all of the forms Ax and x. It follows from Theorem 2.2. that G is regular. Theorem 2.8. is thus valid for connected grammars. We must show that the theorem also holds for grammars which are not connected.

A nonconnected grammar has at least one pair of variables A_i, A_j, for which it is not the case that $A_i \overset{*}{\Rightarrow} \alpha_1 A_j \alpha_2$ for some pair α_1, α_2. We shall prove the theorem for such cases by Mathematical induction, in two steps: (i) we must first show that the theorem is valid for grammars with only one variable, S; (ii) then we assume that it holds for all grammars with less than n variables (the induction-hypothesis) and prove that in that case the theorem also holds for grammars with n variables. It follows from (i) and (ii) that the theorem holds for all grammars with one or more variables.
(i) G has only one variable, S. The only possible pair of variables is thus S,S, and consequently there is no pair α_1 and α_2 such that $S \overset{*}{\Rightarrow} \alpha_1 S \alpha_2$. Since all productions are of the form $S \rightarrow x$, language $L(G)$ is finite; on the basis of Theorem 2.3. it is regular. The theorem is thus valid for nonconnected grammars with one variable.
(ii) Let us assume that the theorem is valid for all grammars with

less than n variables (the induction-hypothesis). Take grammar G with n variables $A_1, A_2, \ldots, A_n$, where $S = A_1$. Because S is the start symbol, it is true for all variables which may occur in the derivation of a sentence (we suppose without loss of generality that G contains no "dummy" variables from which no derivation is possible) that $S \overset{*}{\Rightarrow} \varphi_1 A_j \varphi_2$ $(j > 1)$ and for strings φ_1 and φ_2 in V^*. Because G is not connected, there must be a variable A_i such that it is not true that $A_i \overset{*}{\Rightarrow} \alpha_1 S \alpha_2$ for a pair α_1, α_2. Otherwise we would have $A_i \overset{*}{\Rightarrow} \alpha_1 \varphi_1 A_j \varphi_2 \alpha_2$, but we know that there is at least one pair A_i, A_j for which this is not the case.

Let us first examine the case where $i > 1$, that is, where $A_i \neq S$. We can construct a grammar G' with $n - 1$ variables by removing all productions of the form $A_i \rightarrow \psi$ from G, and by replacing A_i in all productions with a new terminal element a. From the induction-hypothesis it follows that $L(G')$ is regular. Next let us examine the set K of terminal strings x for which $A_i \overset{*}{\Rightarrow} x$ in G, $K = \{x | A_i \overset{*}{\Rightarrow} x\}$. This set can be generated by a grammar G'' which includes all the productions of G except those containing S ($A_i \overset{*}{\Rightarrow} \alpha_1 S \alpha_2$ is impossible), and with A_i as start symbol. Because G'' has fewer than n variables, K is regular (by the induction-hypothesis). $L(G)$, however, is precisely the language which results from the replacement of the element a in the strings of $L(G')$ with strings x from K. It follows from the lemma that $L(G)$ is regular.

Let us now consider the case where $A_i = S$. Take the productions in G of the form $S \rightarrow \alpha$; an arbitrary α_i can be rewritten as a string of terminal and/or nonterminal elements $\xi_1, \xi_2, \ldots, \xi_m$. For each ξ_j in α_i we can define a set of strings L_j for which $\xi_j \overset{*}{\Rightarrow} x$ on the basis of the productions in G. Thus $L_j = \{x | \xi_j \overset{*}{\Rightarrow} x\}$. From the induction-hypothesis it follows that L_j is regular for all j's. Let K_i be the set of strings y for which $\alpha_i \overset{*}{\Rightarrow} y$, i.e. $K_i = \{y | \alpha_i \overset{*}{\Rightarrow} y\}$. From the composition of α_i it follows that each y consists of a sequence of x's respectively taken from $L_1, L_2, \ldots, L_m$, all of which are regular. From Theorem 2.5. it then follows that K_i is regular. $L(G)$ is the union of all K_i's. As a consequence of Theorem 2.4., therefore, $L(G)$ is itself regular. This completes the proof of Theorem 2.8.

2.3.4. *Ambiguity*

The generation of a sentence by a context-free grammar can be represented by a tree diagram. This however does not mean that a given tree diagram corresponds to only one way in which a sentence can be derived.

EXAMPLE 2.5. Let G be a context-free grammar with the following productions:

1. $S \to AB$	5. $B \to Sd$
2. $S \to CD$	6. $C \to aS$
3. $S \to bc$	7. $D \to d$
4. $A \to a$	

The sentence *abcd* can be derived from this grammar as follows: $S \Rightarrow AB \Rightarrow aB \Rightarrow aSd \Rightarrow abcd$. The corresponding derivation tree is shown in Figure 2.4. There are, however, other derivations of *abcd* which correspond to the same tree, for example, the derivation $S \Rightarrow AB \Rightarrow ASd \Rightarrow Abcd \Rightarrow abcd$, where the productions are applied in a different order. This cannot be detected in the tree diagram, which fact corresponds to our intuition that the two derivations determine the same syntactic structure. Therefore we cannot consider this to be a case of real ambiguity.

In order to define ambiguity in terms of derivations, we must introduce the concept of LEFTMOST DERIVATION. We can speak of a leftmost derivation of x if at each step in the derivation $S \overset{*}{\Rightarrow} x$ it is the variable farthest to the left of the string which is rewritten. A leftmost derivation of the sentence *abcd* can begin with $S \Rightarrow AB$. At this stage the leftmost variable is A; thus the following step will be $AB \Rightarrow aB$. The leftmost variable is now B, and the next

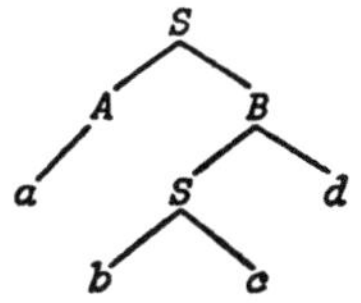

Fig. 2.4. Derivation Tree for the Sentence *abcd* (Example 2.5.).

step is $aB \Rightarrow aSd$, and the final step, $aSd \Rightarrow abcd$. The first derivation given in this example was in fact a leftmost derivation. It is clear that every tree diagram corresponds to no more than one leftmost derivation, and every leftmost derivation with only one tree diagram.

A grammar G is AMBIGUOUS if there is a sentence in $L(G)$ for which there are two or more leftmost derivations.

The grammar given in Example 2.5. is ambiguous, for sentence *abcd* has another leftmost derivation: $S \Rightarrow CD \Rightarrow aSD \Rightarrow abcD \Rightarrow abcd$. The tree diagram for this derivation is shown in Figure 2.5.

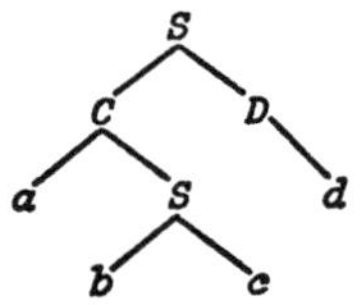

Fig. 2.5. Alternative Derivation Tree for the Sentence *abcd* (Example 2.5.).

A language L is (inherently) ambiguous if all grammars which generate it are ambiguous.

Although grammar G of Example 2.5. is ambiguous, $L(G)$ is not. Language $L(G)$ consists of sentences a^*bcd^*, which can be generated by grammar G' with productions $S \rightarrow aSd$ and $S \rightarrow bc$; G' is not ambiguous. Languages exist, however, which are inherently ambiguous. An example is the union of $\{a^ib^ic^j\}$ and $\{a^ib^jc^j\}$, briefly noted $L = \{a^ib^jc^k | i = j \text{ or } j = k, \text{ where } i, j, k > 1\}$. Any grammar for L will generate sentences with $i = j$ by a different process than sentences with $j = k$. But then sentences with $i = j = k$ can be generated by both processes.

2.3.5. *Linear Grammars*

A production is called LINEAR if it is of the form $A \rightarrow xBy$, i.e. if the string derived contains only one variable. A RIGHT-LINEAR production has the form $A \rightarrow xB$; a LEFT-LINEAR production has the form $A \rightarrow Bx$.

A grammar is linear if each of its productions is either linear or of the form $A \rightarrow x$; a grammar is right-linear if each of its productions is either right-linear or of the form $A \rightarrow x$; a grammar is left-linear if each of its productions is either left-linear or of the form $A \rightarrow x$.

It follows from Theorem 2.1. that a right-linear grammar generates a regular language. Left-linear grammars also generate only regular languages.

An example of a linear grammar is G' mentioned in the preceding paragraph, with productions $S \rightarrow aSd$ and $S \rightarrow bc$. The language generated by it, $\{a^*bcd^*\}$, is not regular; it is therefore self-embedding. Although the class of linear grammars has a greater generative capacity than the class of regular grammars, it does not coincide with the class of context-free languages.

THEOREM 2.9. There are context-free languages for which no linear grammar exists.

For proof of this theorem we refer the reader to Chomsky and Schützenberger (1963). An example of a context-free language for which no linear grammar can be found is language L with sentences $a^{m_1}b^{m_1}a^{m_2}b^{m_2} \ldots a^{m_k}b^{m_k}b$, where $m_i \geqslant 1$ and $k \geqslant 1$, thus strings of alternating sequences of a's and b's, where each sequence of b's is as long as the sequence of a's which precedes it, and ending in a single b. A grammar for this language has the productions $S \rightarrow aSS$, $S \rightarrow b$. The first of these productions is not linear. All other grammars for this language likewise have at least one nonlinear production.

2.4. CONTEXT-SENSITIVE GRAMMARS

2.4.1. *Context-sensitive Productions*

The definition of context-sensitive grammars (grammars in which all productions are of the form $\alpha \rightarrow \beta$, where $|\alpha| \leqslant |\beta|$) does not indicate in what way such grammars are "sensitive to context".

The original definition given by Chomsky (1959a) was in fact different from the present one. He defined context-sensitive grammars (*CSG*) as grammars the productions of which have the form $\alpha_1 A \alpha_2 \to \alpha_1 \beta \alpha_2$, where α_1 and α_2 are elements of V^*, and β is an element of V^+. Thus A can be replaced by β only if A appears in the context $\alpha_1 - \alpha_2$. This type of context-sensitive production can also be written as $A \to \beta / \alpha_1 - \alpha_2$. In spite of the change of definition, the following theorem remains valid.

THEOREM 2.10. The class of languages generated by grammars exclusively containing context-sensitive productions is the class of type-1 languages.

PROOF. Let G_1 be a type-1 grammar, and G_c be a grammar exclusively containing context-sensitive productions. Every G_c is evidently also a G_1, because for all productions $\alpha \to \beta$ in G_c it is true that $|\alpha| \leqslant |\beta|$. However it must likewise be shown that for every G_1 there is an equivalent G_c.

Let $G_1 = (V_N, V_T, P, S)$ be a type-1 grammar. There is a grammar $G' = (V'_N, V'_T, P', S')$ equivalent to it, where all the productions $\alpha \to \beta$ in P' have the following "normal-form": either both α and β are strings exclusively containing variables, or α and β are of the forms A and a respectively (i.e. the productions are of the type $A \to a$). This will become evident from the following. Let V'_N consist of all the elements in V_N as well as an additional variable X_a for each element a in V_T, thus $V'_N = V_N \cup \{X_a | a \in V_T\}$. To compose P' we must change the productions of P in such a way that every terminal element a in them is replaced by X_a, then add productions $X_a \to a$ for every a in V_T. Thus all productions in P' are of the "normal-form" (note that this normal-form can also be used for all type-0 grammars), and $L(G') = L(G_1)$.

We must now find a grammar G'' which contains only context-sensitive productions, and is equivalent to G'. Let $\alpha \to \beta$ be a production in P', with $\alpha = A_1 A_2 \dots A_m$, and $\beta = B_1 B_2 \dots B_n$, where $n \geqslant m$. We replace this production with the following set of equivalent context-sensitive productions in P'':

$$
\begin{array}{lcl}
A_1 \to A_1' \;/\; — A_2A_3 \ldots A_m & & A_1' \to B_1 \\
A_2 \to A_2' \;/\; A_1' — A_3 \ldots A_m & \text{and} & A_2' \to B_2 \\
\vdots & & \vdots \\
A_m \to A_m' \;/\; A_1' \ldots A_{m+1}' — & & A_m' \to B_mB_{m+1} \ldots B_n
\end{array}
$$

The first group of context-sensitive productions (A_1 though A_m) replaces $\alpha = A_1A_2 \ldots A_m$ to a string of new variables $A_1'A_2' \ldots A_m'$. This can in turn be replaced by $B_1B_2 \ldots B_n$ by way of the second group of context-sensitive productions (A_1' through A_m') if $n \geqslant m$. When all the productions of P' have been replaced in this way by sets of context-sensitive productions, and V_N'' includes V_N' and the newly introduced variables, then G'' is equivalent to G' and consequently also to G'. G'', however, is a G_c.

EXAMPLE 2.6. The production $CD \to DC$ is of type-1 form. Application of the procedure mentioned above yields the following set of context-sensitive productions equivalent to $CD \to DC$:

1. $C \to C'/—D$
2. $D \to D'/C'—$
3. $C' \to D$
4. $D' \to C$

An advantage of a type-1 grammar in context-sensitive form (that is, containing productions exclusively in context-sensitive form) is that the derivation of a sentence in it can be represented by means of a tree diagram. Context-sensitive productions, in effect, replace only one variable in the string at each step; each step, therefore, corresponds to the branches leaving only one node. This will be illustrated by the following example.

EXAMPLE 2.7. Let us examine the derivation of sentence *aabbccdd* in grammar G of Example 1.5. G contains the following productions:

1. $S \to ESF$
2. $S \to abcd$
3. $Ea \to aE$
4. $dF \to Fd$
5. $Eb \to abb$
6. $cF \to ccd$

As a first step we replace grammar G with grammar G', containing the following "normal form" productions, obtained by application of the procedure explained in the proof of Theorem 2.10.:

1. $S \to ESF$	6. $X_b \to b$
2. $S \to X_aX_bX_cX_d$	7. $EX_b \to X_aX_bX_b$
3. $EX_a \to X_aE$	8. $X_cF \to X_cX_cX_d$
4. $X_a \to a$	9. $X_c \to c$
5. $X_dF \to FX_d$	10. $X_d \to d$

The productions are now replaced by context-sensitive productions where necessary by application of the procedure given in Example 2.6. This yields the following productions; productions 3-6 and 8-11 were obtained by means of this procedure:

1. $S \to ESF$	9. $X_d \to X'_d \,/\, — F'$
2. $S \to X_aX_bX_cX_d$	10. $F' \to X_d$
3. $E \to E' \,/\, — X_a$	11. $X'_d \to F$
4. $X_a \to X'_a \,/\, E'—$	12. $X_b \to b$
5. $E' \to X_a$	13. $E \to X_aX_b \,/\, — X_b$
6. $X'_a \to E$	14. $F \to X_cX_d \,/\, X_c —$
7. $X_a \to a$	15. $X_c \to c$
8. $F \to F' \,/\, X_d—$	16. $X_d \to d$

These productions can be used to derive the sentence *aabbccdd* in the following way (the numbers over the arrows refer to the productions applied):

$$S \overset{1}{\Rightarrow} ESF \overset{2}{\Rightarrow} EX_aX_bX_cX_dF \overset{3}{\Rightarrow} E'X_aX_bX_cX_dF$$
$$\overset{4}{\Rightarrow} E'X'_aX_bX_cX_dF \overset{5}{\Rightarrow} X_aX'_aX_bX_cX_dF \overset{6}{\Rightarrow} X_aEX_bX_cX_dF$$
$$\overset{8}{\Rightarrow} X_aEX_bX_cX_dF' \overset{9}{\Rightarrow} X_aEX_bX_cX'_dF' \overset{10}{\Rightarrow} X_aEX_bX_cX'_dX_d$$
$$\overset{11}{\Rightarrow} X_aEX_bX_cFX_d \overset{13}{\Rightarrow} X_aX_aX_bX_bX_cFX_d \overset{14}{\Rightarrow} X_aX_aX_bX_bX_cX_cX_dX_d$$
$$\xrightarrow{7,\,12,\,15,\,16} aabbccdd.$$

All sixteen productions have been used in this derivation. Figure 2.6., gives the corresponding tree diagram.

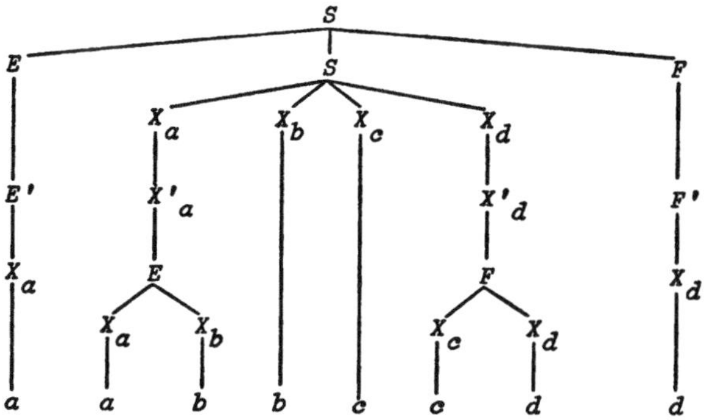

Fig. 2.6. Derivation Tree for the Sentence *aabbccdd* (Example 2.7.).

Nevertheless, tree diagrams for derivations in context-sensitive grammars are less exhaustive in illustrating the precise steps of derivation than tree diagrams for derivations in context-free grammars. More specifically, the diagrams do not show the contextual restrictions operative at the various steps of rewriting in a context-sensitive grammar, and it is possible that two derivations, based on different sets of productions, will be represented by the same tree diagram. For a context-sensitive derivation, as opposed to a context-free derivation, the "ambiguity of x" does not correspond to "more than one possible tree diagram for x".

2.4.2. *The Kuroda Normal-Form*

In the preceding paragraph two restricted forms of context-sensitive productions were discussed; they may be called normal-forms. The first of them contains two types of production, $\alpha \rightarrow \beta$ with α and β in V_N^+ and $|\alpha| \leqslant |\beta|$, and $A \rightarrow a$. The second is the context-sensitive form $A \rightarrow \beta/\alpha_1 - \alpha_2$, with α_1 and α_2 in V^* and β in V^+. We shall now introduce a third normal-form, developed by Kuroda, which is relevant not only to the discussion of the relationship between context-sensitive grammars and automata (chapter 6), but also to the proof of certain essential properties of transformational grammars (Volume II, chapter 5).

THEOREM 2.11. Every context-sensitive grammar is equivalent to a context-sensitive grammar with productions exclusively in the following forms:

(i) $S \rightarrow SB$, (ii) $CD \rightarrow EF$, (iii) $G \rightarrow H$, (iv) $A \rightarrow a$, where the variables A, B, C, D, E, F, and H are different from the start symbol S (G may be identical to S).

PROOF. It is striking that no string in these production forms has more than two elements. We shall first show that if G is context-sensitive, there exists a grammar G' equivalent to it, in which for each production $\alpha \rightarrow \beta$, $|\alpha| \leqslant 2$, and $|\beta| \leqslant 2$. In the second place we will prove that there is a grammar G_n in the Kuroda normal-form which is equivalent to G'.

Let $G = (V_N, V_T, P, S)$ be a context-sensitive grammar. We already know that there is an equivalent grammar G'' of the first normal-form, i.e. with production types $A \rightarrow a$ and $\alpha \rightarrow \beta$, where α and β are strings of variables such that $|\beta| \geqslant |\alpha| > 0$. Suppose that the maximum length of any string of a production of G'' is n. We must construct a grammar $G''' = (V_N''', V_T, P''', S)$ equivalent to G'' (and thus also to G), for which the maximum string length for any production is not greater than $n - 1$. To do so, we let P''' include all the productions of P'' where the string length is no greater than 2; the remaining productions have string lengths of 3 or more. (If $n = 1$ or $n = 2$, G'' already conforms to the limitation on string length and this step may be omitted.) Let $\alpha \rightarrow \beta$ be such a production; we write it then as

$$A\alpha' \rightarrow BCD\beta' \text{ (where } |\alpha'| \geqslant 0 \text{ and } |\beta'| \geqslant 0).$$

If $\alpha' = \lambda$, we create two new variables A_1 and A_2, and add the following productions to P''':

$$A \rightarrow A_1A_2$$
$$A_1 \rightarrow BC$$
$$A_2 \rightarrow D\beta'$$

If $|\alpha'| > 0$, α' can be replaced by $E\alpha''$. In that case we add the following productions to P''':

$AE \rightarrow A'E'$
$A' \rightarrow B$
$E'\alpha'' \rightarrow CD\beta'$

It is clear that in both cases no string length is greater than $n - 1$. If we follow this procedure for all the productions of P'' and add the resulting productions to P''', in virtue of the construction G''' will be equivalent to G'', and consequently also to G. By induction on n it follows that there is a grammar $G' = (V'_N, V_T, P', S)$ in which the length of the strings in productions is limited to 2, and which is equivalent to G.

At this point we must show that there is a grammar G_n which is equivalent to G' and G, and which contains only productions of types (i) through (iv). Take grammar $G_n = (V^n_N, V_T, P^n, S')$, where $V^n_N = \{V'_N \cup S' \cup Q\}$. Thus we have added two new variables, one of which, S', is a new start symbol. The productions in P^n are the following:

1. $S' \rightarrow S'Q$
2. $S' \rightarrow S$
3. $QA \rightarrow AQ$ } for all variables A in G'
4. $AQ \rightarrow QA$ }
5. $A \rightarrow B$ for all productions $A \rightarrow B$ in G'
6. $A \rightarrow b$ for all productions $A \rightarrow b$ in G'
7. $AB \rightarrow CD$ for all productions $AB \rightarrow CD$ in G'
8. $AQ \rightarrow BC$ for all productions $A \rightarrow BC$ in G'

It is clear that the productions of G_n are subject to the same restriction of string length as the productions of G'; all strings in productions are of a length no greater than 2. Productions 1 through 8, moreover, are all of types (i) through (iv). (Note that the start symbol is S', while S is an ordinary variable.)

Finally, we must prove that G_n is equivalent to G'; to do so it will be necessary to show that if $x \in L(G_n)$, it is also true that $x \in L(G')$, as well as the inverse. (1) If $x \in L(G_n)$, then $S' \overset{*}{\Rightarrow} x$. When every S' in the derivation is replaced by S and all Q's are omitted, every step of the derivation is in G'. This may be seen when the same operation is performed on the eight productions of G_n. The first and second productions become $S \rightarrow S$ (which adds nothing essential); the third and fourth productions become $A \rightarrow A$ (which is equally uninteresting); the fifth, sixth, and seventh productions remain unchanged, and the eighth production becomes $A \rightarrow BC$. Thus if $S' \overset{*}{\Rightarrow} x$, each step in the derivation of x can be simulated by the application of the productions of G', and therefore it is true that $x \in L(G')$.

(2) Let $x \in L(G')$; then $S \overset{*}{\Rightarrow} x$. It is true of every production $\alpha \rightarrow \beta$ in G' that it is either contained in G_n or has been replaced by a production of type 8, $AQ \rightarrow BC$. Therefore, in order to generate x in G_n we must see to it that there is exactly one Q available for each step of derivation in which a production of the type $A \rightarrow BC$ is involved. The Q must be placed directly to the right of the variable A to be rewritten. This can easily be done in G_n: we first count the number of steps in the derivation $S \overset{*}{\Rightarrow} x$ in which the situation occurs, for instance n times. We then begin the derivation of x in G_n by applying the first production n times; this may be written as $S' \overset{*}{\Rightarrow} S'Q^n$. Next we replace S' with S by means of the second production, thus $S'Q^n \Rightarrow SQ^n$. The rest of the derivation can proceed in the same way as the derivation $S \overset{*}{\Rightarrow} x$, except where the eighth type of production is involved. In this latter case we must move one Q to the position directly to the right of the variable to be rewritten; this is done by application of productions of the third and fourth types. The Q is then eliminated upon application of a production of the eighth type. In this way G_n can generate x.

It follows from (1) and (2) that $L(G_n) = L(G')$. Since G' is equivalent to G, G_n in the Kuroda normal-form is also equivalent to G. This concludes the proof of Theorem 2.11.

We would note in conclusion that Kuroda called his normal-form a "linear bounded grammar", analogous to the equivalent automaton of the same name (cf. chapter 6).

3

PROBABILISTIC GRAMMARS

3.1. DEFINITIONS AND CONCEPTS

Until now we have limited the concept of grammar to a system of rules according to which the sentences of a language may be generated. On the basis of such a concept one can distinguish differences in the sentences of a language only in their derivation, also called their STRUCTURAL DESCRIPTION. However one might also consider the differences in frequency with which sentence types occur in a language. One reason for doing so, as we shall see in chapter 8, is to facilitate the choice between two or more grammars which generate the same language. One might determine the efficiency of a grammar on the basis of the frequencies with which particular derivations or sentence types occur in a language. But the concept "efficiency" has not been clearly defined, and the usefulness of a probabilistic interpretation of it will have to be considered in each concrete situation. We shall return to this subject in chapter 8.

We shall limit our discussion in the present chapter to an extension of the concept "grammar" which will enable us to describe the probability of occurrence of sentences in a language. Therefore, we shall first define the concept of a probabilistic grammar.

A PROBABILISTIC GRAMMAR G is a system (V_N, V_T, P, S) in which:

(1) V_N (the nonterminal vocabulary), V_T (the terminal vocabulary), and P (the productions) are finite, nonempty sets.

(2) $V_N \cap V_T = \emptyset$.

(3) Let $V_N \cup V_T = V$; P is composed of ordered groups of three elements $(\alpha_i, \beta_j, p_{ij})$, ordinarily written $\alpha_i \overset{p_{ij}}{\rightarrow} \beta_j$, where $\alpha_i \in V^+$, $\beta_j \in V^*$, and p_{ij} is a real number indicating the probability that a given string α_i will be rewritten as β_j. The number p_{ij} is called the PRODUCTION PROBABILITY of $\alpha_i \rightarrow \beta_j$.

(4) $S \in V_N$.

This definition differs from the original definition of grammar only in that a probability is assigned to every production.

A probabilistic grammar is NORMALIZED if for every production $\alpha_i \overset{p_{ij}}{\rightarrow} \beta_j$, it is true that $\sum_j p_{ij} = 1$ for every α_i in the productions. This means that if α_i occurs in a derivation, the total chance that α_i will be rewritten by means of some production is equal to 1. A production whose probability is equal to 0 cannot be used; it can simply be excluded from P. The reason for allowing the possibility that $p = 0$ is only of practical interest in some calculations. In the following, however, we shall suppose that every $p_{ij} > 0$ unless otherwise mentioned.

We use the notation $\alpha \overset{p}{\underset{*}{\Rightarrow}} \beta$ for a derivation $\alpha \overset{p_1}{\Rightarrow} \xi_1 \overset{p_2}{\Rightarrow} \xi_2 \dots \overset{p_n}{\Rightarrow} \beta$, where each step is the result of the application of one production, and where $p = f(p_1, p_2, \dots, p_n)$. The analogy with standard notation is obvious, but to avoid crowding symbols above the arrow, we shall omit the asterisk, except where doing so might lead to confusion, and write $\alpha \overset{p}{\Rightarrow} \beta$.

Function f is determined by the interdependence, or lack of it, between the various steps of the derivation. A probabilistic grammar is called UNRESTRICTED if the steps of a derivation in it are mutually independent; in this case $p = p_1 \cdot p_2 \cdot \dots \cdot p_n$. As no considerable literature exists on the subject of restricted probabilistic grammars, we shall limit our discussion to unrestricted probabilistic grammars. In applications of the theory, however, it will be necessary to estimate the validity of the presupposition that the productions are mutually independent.

A SENTENCE generated by a probabilistic grammar is a finite string s of terminal elements, where $S \overset{p}{\Rightarrow} s$ and $p > 0$.

A probabilistic grammar G is AMBIGUOUS if at least one sentence can be derived in it in more than one way. A sentence is k-times ambiguous if there are k derivations $S \overset{p_1}{\Rightarrow} s$, $S \overset{p_2}{\Rightarrow} s$, ..., $S \overset{p_k}{\Rightarrow} s$.

A PROBABILISTIC LANGUAGE L, generated by a probabilistic grammar G, is the set of pairs $(s, p(s))$, where: (1) s is a sentence generated by G, and (2) $p(s) = \sum_{i=1}^{k} p_i(s)$ where k is the number of different ways in which s can be derived from S. We call $p(s)$ the PROBABILITY of s in L. A probabilistic language can also be defined, without reference to a grammar, as a subset of V_T^* for which a probability distribution has been defined (V_T is any finite vocabulary).

Two probabilistic grammars G_1 and G_2 are EQUIVALENT if they generate the same probabilistic language L, i.e. the same set of pairs $(s, p(s))$. Notice that equivalence here requires also that the probabilities of the sentences be the same.

A probabilistic language $L = \{(s, p(s))\}$ is NORMALIZED if $\sum_{s \in L} p(s) = 1$. This means that the language has a total probability of 1. We shall see later that a normalized probabilistic grammar need not generate a normalized probabilistic language.

3.2. CLASSIFICATION

Probabilistic grammars may be classified as follows in a way completely analogous to that used in Chapter 2.

Type-0 probabilistic grammars are all probabilistic grammars which satisfy the definition given above. Type-1 or CONTEXT-SENSITIVE probabilistic grammars are those probabilistic grammars in which, for all productions $\alpha_i \overset{p_{ij}}{\rightarrow} \beta_j$, it is true that $|\alpha_i| \leqslant |\beta_j|$. Type-2 or CONTEXT-FREE probabilistic grammars are those probabilistic grammars in which, for all productions $\alpha_i \overset{p_{ij}}{\rightarrow} \beta_j$, it is true that $\alpha_i = A_i \in V_N$. Type-3 or REGULAR probabilistic grammars are type-2 probabilistic grammars whose productions are exclusively of the forms $A \overset{p}{\rightarrow} aB$ and $A \overset{p}{\rightarrow} a$.

It is obvious that this classification is completely independent of the probabilistic aspect of the grammars. This is also true of the classification of probabilistic LANGUAGES generated by probabilistic grammars. Thus we have type-0 probabilistic languages, type-1 or context-sensitive probabilistic languages, type-2 or context-free probabilistic languages, and type-3 or regular probabilistic languages.

In the present chapter only regular and context-free probabilistic grammars will be treated, as no results on the other two types are yet available.

3.3. REGULAR PROBABILISTIC GRAMMARS

Three theorems will be treated in this paragraph. The first of them is of direct practical interest. The second, on the other hand, appears to be somewhat alarming from a practical point of view, but the third, which has not as yet been proven, suggests that things might not be as problematic as they seem.

THEOREM 3.1. Every normalized regular probabilistic grammar generates a normalized regular probabilistic language.

In such a case, the probabilistic grammar is said to be CONSISTENT, and the theorem is therefore called a CONSISTENCY-THEOREM.

The theorem is of practical interest in determining the frequencies of sentences in a language. To do so one would wish to be certain that the sum of the corresponding probabilisties is equal to 1. The theorem states that this is guaranteed if the regular grammar in question is normalized.

The proof of this theorem supposes some acquaintance with matrix algebra. For readers who prefer to omit it we shall first present an example which holds the essence of the proof without requiring knowledge of matrix algebra. The general proof will be given later.

EXAMPLE 3.1. Let G be a regular probabilistic grammar with the following productions:

1. $S \xrightarrow{1/2} a$
2. $S \xrightarrow{1/2} aB$
3. $B \xrightarrow{1/3} bA$
4. $B \xrightarrow{2/3} b$
5. $A \xrightarrow{1} a$

G is normalized because for every variable the total chance of being rewritten is equal to 1. Only three sentences can be generated by G: *a*, *ab*, *aba*. The derivations with their respective probabilities are as follows:

$$S \overset{1/2}{\Rightarrow} a \quad \ldots\ldots \quad p(a) = \tfrac{1}{2}$$

$$S \overset{1/2}{\Rightarrow} aB \overset{2/3}{\Rightarrow} ab \quad \ldots\ldots \quad p(ab) = \tfrac{1}{2} \cdot \tfrac{2}{3} = \tfrac{1}{3}$$

$$S \overset{1/2}{\Rightarrow} aB \overset{1/3}{\Rightarrow} abA \overset{1}{\Rightarrow} aba \quad \ldots\ldots \quad p(aba) = \tfrac{1}{2} \cdot \tfrac{1}{3} \cdot 1 = \tfrac{1}{6}$$

$L(G)$ is evidently normalized, because $\sum_{s \in L(G)} p(s) = \frac{1}{2} + \frac{1}{3} + \frac{1}{6} = 1.$ On the basis of this example we shall now show that there is a simple method for determining the chance that a regular probabilistic grammar will generate sentences up to a certain length. To do so we present the probabilities of the productions in G in matrix form [1] as follows:

	S	A	B	V_T
S	0	0	$\frac{1}{2}$	$\frac{1}{2}$
A	0	0	0	1
B	0	$\frac{1}{3}$	0	$\frac{2}{3}$
V_T	0	0	0	1

$= C$

Let us examine the first row (row-element S). It shows the chances for the respective column-elements to appear in direct or "one-

[1] A matrix is a rectangular grid with one or more rows and one or more columns. Each row is denoted by a ROW-ELEMENT x_i, and each column by a COLUMN-ELEMENT y_i. At the intersection of row i and column j is the MATRIX-ELEMENT a_{ij}.

step" derivations from S. There are only two productions for rewriting S, $S \xrightarrow{\frac{1}{2}} aB$ and $S \xrightarrow{\frac{1}{2}} a$. The matrix-element under B in row S has the value $\frac{1}{2}$ because of the first of these productions, and the matrix-element under V_T in the same row has the value $\frac{1}{2}$ because of the second production. Column V_T thus serves for all productions in which a variable is rewritten as a terminal element, regardless of which terminal element it is. Row A shows how the variable A can be rewritten in one step, and with what probability, thus A can be rewritten only as a terminal element, with probability 1. Row B shows to which elements the variable B can be rewritten, and with what probability, thus it can be rewritten as A with probability $\frac{1}{3}$ and as a terminal element with probability $\frac{2}{3}$. The fourth row, row V_T, is added to the matrix for further calculations; it is composed of zeros, except the rightmost element which has the value 1.

This matrix, which we shall call matrix C, has a pleasant property which may be explained as follows. We know that by definition sentences are derived from S. If we wish to know the chance for a sentence with length 1, we look at row S under V_T, and find the value $\frac{1}{2}$. What then is the chance for a sentence of length 1 or 2? Such sentences are derived by going from S to V_T by two steps at most. The variables S, A, or B may be present in the first derived string. Consequently there are four possibilities of arriving at a sentence with a length of 2:

(1) From S a string is derived in which S is present, then S is replaced by a terminal element. One can immediately see in the matrix that these two steps have respective probabilities of 0 and $\frac{1}{2}$. The total chance of such a derivation is thus $0 \cdot \frac{1}{2} = 0$.

(2) From S the variable A is first derived, then a terminal element is derived from A. The chance for this is $0 \cdot 1 = 0$.

(3) From S a string is derived with the variable B, then a terminal element is derived from B. The chance for this is $\frac{1}{2} \cdot \frac{2}{3} = \frac{1}{3}$.

(4) A terminal element is directly derived from S. The chance for this is $\frac{1}{2}$. The total chance for a sentence with length 1 or 2 is the

sum of these four probabilities, $0 + 0 + \frac{1}{3} + \frac{1}{2} = \frac{5}{6}$. This is precisely the chance for the sentence *a* ($\frac{1}{2}$) plus the chance for the sentence *ab* ($\frac{1}{3}$), the only two sentences of the grammar in this category.

This operation can also be carried out systematically by means of MATRIX-MULTIPLICATION. The four steps which we have just performed correspond to the multiplication in pairs of the elements in row S with the elements in column V_T, followed by the addition of the four products: $(0 \cdot \frac{1}{2}) + (0 \cdot 1) + (\frac{1}{2} \cdot \frac{2}{3}) + (\frac{1}{2} \cdot 1) = \frac{5}{6}$. We say then that the row-vector S is multiplied by the column-vector V_T. Let us make a new matrix C^2, and put the result $\frac{5}{6}$ at the intersection of row S and column V_T. The remaining matrix-elements of C^2 are obtained in a similar way, that is the multiplication of a given row-vector in C with a given column-vector in C yields the matrix-element in C^2 for the intersection of the row and column in question. For example, the matrix-element in C^2 for the intersection of row S and column A is $\frac{1}{6}$. This is obtained by multiplying the row-vector S in C by the column-vector A: $(0 \cdot 0) + (0 \cdot 0) + (\frac{1}{2} \cdot \frac{1}{3}) + (\frac{1}{2} \cdot 0) = \frac{1}{6}$. The value $\frac{1}{6}$ means that there is one chance out of six of deriving a string with A from S in no more than two steps. Matrix C^2 is called the square of matrix C.

	S	A	B	V_T	
S	0	$\frac{1}{6}$	0	$\frac{5}{6}$	
A	0	0	0	1	$= C^2$
B	0	0	0	1	
V_T	0	0	0	1	

By multiplying C by C^2 (multiplying the row-vectors in C by the column-vectors in C^2) we obtain matrix C^3:

	S	A	B	V_T	
S	0	0	0	1	
A	0	0	0	1	$= C^3$
B	0	0	0	1	
V_T	0	0	0	1	

In row S under V_T we find the value 1. This means that the chance of obtaining a sentence the length of which is three or smaller is equal to 1. The grammar, as we have observed, generates no longer sentences.

In this example we see that the critical matrix-element in row S under V_T increases with the power of the matrix from $\frac{1}{2}$ to $\frac{5}{6}$ to 1. The proof of Theorem 3.1 consists of showing that this is a generally valid theorem for matrices such as matrix C. By increasing the power of the matrix, i.e. the sentence length, the critical element approaches the value 1. The sum of the chances for all sentences, i.e. for the sentences of all lengths, is thus equal to 1, and $L(G)$ is normalized.

PROOF. Let G be a normalized regular probabilistic grammar. We suppose that G has no redundant variables, i.e. for each $A \in V_N$ there is at least one production $A \xrightarrow{p} a$, $a \in V_T$, for which $p > 0$. This supposition implies no loss of generality (cf. Huang and Fu 1971). Let us define a matrix $C = [c_{ij}]$, $i, j = 1, 2, \ldots, n+1$, as follows:

$$c_{ij} = \sum_{a \in V_T} p(A_i \to aA_j)$$ for $i, j \leqslant n$, and where p is the production probability of $A_i \to aA_j$.

$$c_{ij} = \sum_{a \in V_T} p(A_i \to a)$$ for $i \leqslant n, j = n+1$

$$c_{ij} = 0$$ for $i = n+1, j \leqslant n$

$$c_{n+1,n+1} = 1$$

C is a stochastic matrix [1] because for each row the sum of the elements is equal to 1, and G is normalized. The right hand column-vector in matrix C^k shows the probability that a string of k or fewer elements will be derived from the variable A_i. If $A_1 = S$, then $c^k_{1,n+1}$ is the probability that the grammar generates a sentence of k or fewer elements. We are interested in the value of $c^k_{1,n+1}$ when $k \to \infty$, i.e. the sum of the probabilities of all sentences

[1] A STOCHASTIC MATRIX is a square matrix, the matrix-elements of which are not negative, and the sums of the rows of which are equal to 1 (cf. Feller 1968).

generated by the grammar. We have supposed that it is true of every variable A that $\sum_{a \in V_T} p(A \to a) > 0$, that is, that there are no redundant variables. C may therefore be written as $C = \begin{bmatrix} A & B \\ 0 & 1 \end{bmatrix}$, where all the elements of column-vector B have a value > 0. Then $C^2 = \begin{bmatrix} A^2 & AB+B \\ 0 & 1 \end{bmatrix}$, and in general, $C^k = \begin{bmatrix} A^k & (A^{k-1}+A^{k-2}...A^{\circ})B \\ 0 & 1 \end{bmatrix}$ $= \begin{bmatrix} A^k & D \\ 0 & 1 \end{bmatrix}$. But for each of the row-vectors in A, the sum of the row-elements is smaller than 1, and consequently $\lim_{k \to \infty} A^k = 0$. But C^n is a stochastic matrix because C is a stochastic matrix (this theorem is treated in Feller 1968), and thus for every row in C^k the sum of the row elements is also equal to 1. The limit of each of the row-vectors in C^k is thus [0 0 ... 0 1], and thus $\lim_{k \to \infty} c_{1,n+1} = 1$ is what we set out to prove.

A normalized regular grammar generates a normalized regular language. But let us examine the situation from the other side. Let L be a regular language for which a probability distribution has been defined. There is thus a value $p(s)$ for every s in L. Let us suppose that L is normalized, i.e. that $\sum_{s \in L} p(s) = 1$. Is there a regular probabilistic grammar which generates precisely the pairs $(s, p(s))$? This is known as the PROBLEM OF REPRESENTATION. We have the following theorem.

THEOREM 3.2. There is a regular language L, and a probability distribution for the sentences in L with the property $\sum_{s \in L} p(s) = 1$, for which no regular probabilistic grammar exists.

There are thus normalized regular probabilistic languages for which no normalized regular probabilistic grammar exists. The practical implication seems to be that not every sample (corpus) of sentences of a regular language can be described by a regular probabilistic grammar. However, the proof of this theorem, for which reference is made to Ellis (1969), is based on an argument which is completely without practical implications. It is shown, in effect, that one can assign a normalized probability distribution to a regular language such that for some sentences s, $p(s)$ cannot be the product of any production probabilities whatsoever. The argument is based on the consideration that there are real numbers which are not rational. It supposes that some sentences of L have nonrational probabilities, and shows that in certain circumstances it is impossible to represent those probabilities as the product of production probabilities.

In every empirical situation, however, we have to do with samples of the sentences of a language L, and can therefore write the estimates of $p(s)$ as fractions. On the basis of this consideration, Suppes (1970) suggests the following general representation theorem for probabilistic languages; the theorem has not yet been proven.

THEOREM 3.3. If L is a type-i language, and a normalized probability distribution $p(s)$ has been defined for the sentences of L, then there is a type-i normalized probabilistic grammar which generates a probability distribution $p(s)$ for the sentences of L, and for every finite sample S of L the null-hypothesis that S is drawn from $(L, p(s))$ cannot be rejected.

In other words, we can find a probabilistic grammar for every sample (corpus) of sentences, according to which the original probability distribution can be approached so closely that it is impossible to decide (on the basis of a statistical test) if we are dealing with $L(p')$ or with $L(p)$.

3.4. CONTEXT-FREE PROBABILISTIC GRAMMARS

Two normal-forms for context-free grammars were introduced in chapter 2, and it was shown that every context-free grammar is equivalent to a grammar in the Chomsky normal-form and to a grammar in the Greibach normal-form. In the present paragraph we shall show that these equivalences are also valid for context-free probabilistic grammars. Afterwards we shall discuss the consistency-problem for context-free probabilistic grammars.

3.4.1. *Normal-Forms*

Normal-forms pose an additional problem for context-free probabilistic grammars, for not only must the normal-form grammar be equivalent to the original one with respect to the sentences generated, but it must also be equivalent to the original grammar with respect to the probability of the sentences generated. This can be done only by giving the production probabilities in the normal-form grammar a certain relation to those of the original grammar. It is not certain in advance that this can always be done. For the Chomsky normal-form we shall state and derive the relations. The Greibach normal-form will only be mentioned.

THEOREM 3.4. (Chomsky normal-form). Every normalized context-free probabilistic grammar G is equivalent to a normalized context-free grammar, the productions of which are exclusively of the forms $A \xrightarrow{p} BC$ and $A \xrightarrow{p} a$.

PROOF. The proof is carried out in three steps. We first construct a grammar G' equivalent to G, and in which no productions of the form $A \xrightarrow{p} B$ occur. Next we compose a grammar G'' equivalent to G', and in which the productions are exclusively of the forms $A \xrightarrow{p} a$ and $A \xrightarrow{p} B_1 B_2 \ldots B_n$ $(n \geqslant 2)$. Finally we compose G_n in the normal-form, equivalent to G'', and consequently also to G.

(i) Let there be such productions in G of the form $A \xrightarrow{p} B$ that derivations of the form $A \overset{p_1}{\Rightarrow} B_1 \overset{p_2}{\Rightarrow} B_2 \ldots \overset{p_n}{\Rightarrow} B_n \overset{p_{n+1}}{\Longrightarrow} \alpha$, where $\alpha \notin V_N$. We can replace every derivation of this kind by adding a production to P' in the form $A \xrightarrow{p} \alpha$, where

(1) $p = p_1 \cdot p_2 \cdot \ldots \cdot p_{n+1}$

This is only possible where there are no "loops" in such a derivation chain. For these cases we do the following. We speak of a loop when productions of the following form occur in P[1]:

$$A \xrightarrow{p_o} B$$

$$A \xrightarrow{p_i} \alpha_i \qquad i = 1,\ldots,n$$

$$B \xrightarrow{q_o} A$$

$$B \xrightarrow{q_j} \beta_j \qquad j = 1,\ldots,m$$

These productions can be replaced by the following productions in P':

$$A \xrightarrow{r_j} \beta_j \qquad j = 1,\ldots,m$$

$$B \xrightarrow{s_i} \alpha_i \qquad i = 1,\ldots,n$$

$$A \xrightarrow{t_i} \alpha_i \qquad i = 1,\ldots,n$$

$$B \xrightarrow{u_j} \beta_j \qquad j = 1,\ldots,m$$

where,

$$(2)\ r_j = \frac{p_o q_j}{1 - p_o q_j},\ t_i = \frac{p_i}{1 - p_o q_o},\ s_i = \frac{q_o p_i}{1 - p_o q_o},\ u_j = \frac{q_j}{1 - p_o q_o}$$

To show this, let us examine in detail the productions $A \xrightarrow{r_j} \beta_j$ in G'; the derivation for the other three types follows the same pattern. β_j can be derived in G in an infinite number of ways when there is a loop of the form $A \xrightarrow{p_o} B$ and $B \xrightarrow{q_o} A$, thus:

$$A \overset{p_o}{\Rightarrow} B \overset{q_i}{\Rightarrow} \beta_j$$

$$A \overset{p_o}{\Rightarrow} B \overset{q_o}{\Rightarrow} A \overset{p_o}{\Rightarrow} B \overset{q_j}{\Rightarrow} \beta_j$$

$$A \overset{p_o}{\Rightarrow} B \overset{q_o}{\Rightarrow} A \overset{p_o}{\Rightarrow} B \overset{q_o}{\Rightarrow} A \overset{p_o}{\Rightarrow} B \overset{q_j}{\Rightarrow} \beta_j, \text{ etc.}$$

The total probability that β_j be derived from A is thus

[1] Notation: In the following probabilities p always corresponds to productions where A occurs to the left of the arrow, and q corresponds to productions where B occurs to the left of the arrow.

$$p_o q_j + p_o(q_o p_o) q_j + p_o(q_o p_o)^2 q_j + \dots =$$

$$p_o q_j \sum_{n=0}^{\infty} (q_o p_o)^n = \frac{p_o q_j}{1 - p_o q_o}.$$

By the same procedure we can deal with t_i, s_i, and u_j.

By eliminating all loops in this way, we obtain grammar G', equivalent to G, and in which there are no productions of the form $A \xrightarrow{p} B$.

(ii) Grammar G'' will contain all the productions of G' except those of the form $A \xrightarrow{p} \beta$, where β consists of terminal elements and possibly also variables ($|\beta| \geqslant 2$). All these productions are rewritten as productions which contain only variables; there will also be a set of terminal productions. If b_i is a terminal element in the string β, we introduce a new variable B_i in G'', and a new terminal production $B_i \xrightarrow{1} b_i$. In this way all the productions of the form $A \xrightarrow{p} \beta$ are replaced by productions of the form $A \xrightarrow{p} B_1B_2 \dots B_n$. It is clear that with this set of productions $A \overset{p}{\Rightarrow} \beta_i$ in G'', and in general that G'' is equivalent to G'.

(iii) At this point all productions in G'' which are not of the form $A \xrightarrow{p} a$ or $A \xrightarrow{p} BC$ must be reduced to the form $A \xrightarrow{p} BC$. The only productions in question here are those of the form $A \xrightarrow{p} B_1B_2 \dots B_n$ ($n > 2$). We replace each of these productions by a set of new productions as follows:

$$A \xrightarrow{p} B_1D_1$$

$$D_1 \xrightarrow{1} B_2D_2$$

$$\vdots$$

$$D_{n-2} \xrightarrow{1} B_{n-1}B_n$$

where D_i is a new variable (i $= 1, \dots n - 2$).

When G_n contains these new productions and these new variables as well as the productions of G'' of the form $A \rightarrow \beta$ with $|\beta| \leqslant 2$, then G_n is obviously equivalent to G'' and therefore also to G, and moreover G_n is of the Chomsky normal-form.

This proof also shows what the relations must be between the production probabilities of the grammar in the Chomsky normal-form and those of the original grammar. They are found in the proof under (1) and (2).

EXAMPLE 3.2. Let $G = (V_N, V_T, P, S)$ be a context-free probabilistic grammar where $V_N = \{S, A, B\}$, $V_T = \{a,b\}$, and P consists of the following productions:

1. $S \xrightarrow{0.8} aS$	5. $A \xrightarrow{0.1} aA \quad (p_2 = 0.1)$
2. $S \xrightarrow{0.2} ABb$	6. $B \xrightarrow{0.4} A \quad (q_o = 0.4)$
3. $A \xrightarrow{0.5} B \quad (p_o = 0.5)$	7. $B \xrightarrow{0.2} Bb \quad (q_1 = 0.2)$
4. $A \xrightarrow{0.4} a \quad (p_1 = 0.4)$	8. $B \xrightarrow{0.4} b \quad (q_2 = 0.4)$

Grammar G is clearly normalized. To find an equivalent grammar in Chomsky normal-form, we must first construct a grammar G', equivalent to G, and in which the loop $A \xrightarrow{0.5} B$, $B \xrightarrow{0.4} A$ no longer occurs. To do so, we replace productions 3 to 8 with the following eight productions (cf. Proof (i)):

$A \xrightarrow{r_1} Bb$	$A \xrightarrow{t_1} aA$
$A \xrightarrow{r_2} b$	$A \xrightarrow{t_2} a$
$B \xrightarrow{s_1} aA$	$B \xrightarrow{u_1} Bb$
$B \xrightarrow{s_2} a$	$B \xrightarrow{u_2} b$

In order to calculate the values of r, s, t, and u, we use the following formulas:

$$r_1 = \frac{p_o q_1}{1 - p_o q_o} = \frac{0.5 \times 0.2}{1 - 0.5 \times 0.4} = \frac{0.1}{0.8} = 0.125$$

$$r_2 = \frac{p_o q_2}{1 - p_o q_o} = \frac{0.5 \times 0.4}{0.8} = 0.25$$

$$s_1 = \frac{q_o p_2}{1 - p_o q_o} = \frac{0.4 \times 0.1}{0.8} = 0.05$$

$$s_2 = \frac{q_o p_1}{1 - p_o q_o} = \frac{0.4 \times 0.4}{0.8} = 0.2$$

$$t_1 = \frac{p_2}{1 - p_o q_o} = \frac{0.1}{0.8} = 0.125$$

$$t_2 = \frac{p_1}{1 - p_o q_o} = \frac{0.4}{0.8} = 0.5$$

$$u_1 = \frac{q_1}{1 - p_o q_o} = \frac{0.2}{0.8} = 0.25$$

$$u_2 = \frac{q_2}{1 - p_o q_o} = \frac{0.4}{0.8} = 0.5$$

If we add the first and second productions of G to G', grammar G' is equivalent to G.

Grammar G'' is obtained by replacing the productions in G' with productions exclusively of the forms $A \xrightarrow{p} a$ and $A \xrightarrow{p} \beta$, where every β is made up only of variables. This yields the following productions in G'':

$S \xrightarrow{0.8} A_1S$	$A \xrightarrow{0.125} BB_2$	$A_2 \xrightarrow{1} a$	$A \xrightarrow{0.5} a$
$A_1 \xrightarrow{1} a$	$B_2 \xrightarrow{1} b$	$B \xrightarrow{0.2} a$	$B \xrightarrow{0.25} BB_3$
$S \xrightarrow{0.2} ABB_1$	$A \xrightarrow{0.25} b$	$A \xrightarrow{0.125} A_3A$	$B_3 \xrightarrow{1} b$
$B_1 \xrightarrow{1} b$	$B \xrightarrow{0.05} A_2A$	$A_3 \xrightarrow{1} a$	$B \xrightarrow{0.5} b$

Finally, grammar G_n in Chomsky normal-form can be obtained by replacing the production $S \xrightarrow{0.2} ABB_1$ with $S \xrightarrow{0.2} AC$ and $C \xrightarrow{1} BB_1$.

The grammar in Chomsky normal-form will then contain the seventeen following productions:

1. $S \xrightarrow{0.8} A_1S$	6. $A \xrightarrow{0.25} b$	10. $B \xrightarrow{0.25} BB_3$	14. $B_1 \xrightarrow{1} b$
2. $S \xrightarrow{0.2} AC$	7. $A_1 \xrightarrow{1} a$	11. $B \xrightarrow{0.05} A_2A$	15. $B_2 \xrightarrow{1} b$
3. $A \xrightarrow{0.125} BB_2$	8. $A_2 \xrightarrow{1} a$	12. $B \xrightarrow{0.5} b$	16. $B_3 \xrightarrow{1} b$
4. $A \xrightarrow{0.125} A_3A$	9. $A_3 \xrightarrow{1} a$	13. $B \xrightarrow{0.2} a$	17. $C \xrightarrow{1} BB_1$
5. $A \xrightarrow{0.5} a$			

This grammar is clearly normalized. But one cannot immediately see that a sentence generated by G has the same probability as a sentence generated by G_n. This is because every sentence generated by G has an infinity of possible leftmost derivations as a result of the loop. This emphasizes the advantage of a grammar in the Chomsky normal-form, since such a grammar has only a finite number of leftmost derivations for each sentence.

THEOREM 3.5. (Greibach normal-form) Every normalized context-free probabilistic grammar G is equivalent to a normalized context-free probabilistic grammar G', in which all productions are of the form $A \xrightarrow{p} a\alpha$, where $\alpha \in V_N^*$.

For proof of this theorem, as well as for the derivation of the production probabilities, we refer the reader to Huang and Fu (1971).

3.4.2. *Consistency Conditions for Context-free Probabilistic Grammars*

The theorems on the normal-forms tell us something of equivalence for normalized probabilistic grammars. But it is of interest to recall the definition: two normalized grammars may well generate the same probabilistic language, but that need not mean that the language is also normalized. The following theorem shows that one may not take it for granted that a normalized context-free grammar generates a normalized language. Context-free probabilistic grammars are not necessarily consistent.

THEOREM 3.6. (Inconsistency theorem) There are normalized context-free probabilistic grammars which do not generate normalized probabilistic languages.

PROOF. For proof of this theorem it is sufficient to show an example of such a grammar. Let $G = (\{S\}, \{a\}, P, S)$ be a grammar with the following productions in P:

1. $S \xrightarrow{\frac{2}{3}} SS$ 2. $S \xrightarrow{\frac{1}{3}} a.$

This grammar is normalized (and moreover in Chomsky normalform); it generates the language $L = \{a^n\}$, where $n \geqslant 1$. The respective derivations of sentences a and aa are as follows:

$$S \overset{\frac{1}{3}}{\Rightarrow} a \qquad\qquad p(a) = 1/3$$

$$S \overset{\frac{2}{3}}{\Rightarrow} SS \overset{\frac{1}{3}}{\Rightarrow} aS \overset{\frac{1}{3}}{\Rightarrow} aa \qquad\qquad p(a^2) = 2/27$$

For the sentence aaa, there are two leftmost derivations possible:

$$S \overset{\frac{2}{3}}{\Rightarrow} SS \overset{\frac{2}{3}}{\Rightarrow} SSS \overset{\frac{1}{3}}{\Rightarrow} aSS \overset{\frac{1}{3}}{\Rightarrow} aaS \overset{\frac{1}{3}}{\Rightarrow} aaa$$

$$S \overset{\frac{2}{3}}{\Rightarrow} SS \overset{\frac{1}{3}}{\Rightarrow} aS \overset{\frac{2}{3}}{\Rightarrow} aSS \overset{\frac{1}{3}}{\Rightarrow} aaS \overset{\frac{1}{3}}{\Rightarrow} aaa$$

The reader will notice here that these derivations correspond to two different tree diagrams; G is therefore ambiguous. For $p(a^3)$ we find $(\frac{2}{3} \cdot \frac{2}{3} \cdot \frac{1}{3} \cdot \frac{1}{3} \cdot \frac{1}{3}) + (\frac{2}{3} \cdot \frac{1}{3} \cdot \frac{2}{3} \cdot \frac{1}{3} \cdot \frac{1}{3}) = 2 \cdot (\frac{2}{3})^2 \cdot (\frac{1}{3})^3 = \frac{8}{243}$. In general we can state that $p(a^n) = (n-1)\,(\frac{2}{3})^{n-1}\,(\frac{1}{3})^n$, where $n > 1$. After some calculation it appears that $\sum_{n=1}^{\infty} p(a^n) = \frac{1}{2}$, instead of the 1 required for normalization. G is therefore inconsistent.

It is possible, however, to pose conditions under which a normalized context-free probabilistic grammar will be consistent. For the following discussion of such conditions, some acquaintance with matrix algebra will again be required. We would advise readers who wish to omit the remainder of this paragraph that in any case every nonambiguous normalized context-free probabilistic grammar is consistent.

The conditions of consistency for a context-free grammar can best be discussed on the basis of the $n \times n$ matrix $A = [a_{ij}]$. Before defining the elements a_{ij}, we must first indicate what they are to represent. The value a_{ij} must be the total chance that the variable A_i generates at least one A_j in a derivation. Take the following productions for A_i and the corresponding probabilities:

$$\begin{array}{lcl} A_i \to \alpha_1 & & p(A_i \to \alpha_1) \\ A_i \to \alpha_2 & \text{with probabilities} & p(A_i \to \alpha_2) \\ \vdots & & \vdots \\ A_i \to \alpha_k & & p(A_i \to \alpha_k) \end{array}$$

and suppose that in the hth production $A_i \to \alpha_h$, the element A_j appears in the derivation m_{ijh} times. The production will thus be as follows:

$$A_i \to \beta_1 A_j \beta_2 A_j \ldots \beta_{m_{ijh}} A_j \beta_{m_{ijh}+1},$$
where $|\beta_l| \geqslant 0$ for $l = 1, \ldots, m_{ijh}+1$.

We define a_{ijh} as follows: $a_{ijh} = m_{ijh} \cdot p(A \to \alpha_h)$. The definition of a_{ij} is then: $a_{ij} = \sum_{h=1}^{k} a_{ijh}$, with $i, j = 1, 2, \ldots, N$, where N is the number of variables in V_N.

In order to construct a consistent context-free probabilistic grammar, we must see to it that $\lim_{n\to\infty} A^n = 0$. This means that finally every variable, and consequently also $A_1 = S$, is rewritten as a terminal element. From this point of view, matrix A here fulfills precisely the same function as matrix C in the proof of Theorem 3.1. It is established (cf. Booth 1969, for example) that the limit is equal to the null-matrix 0, when the eigenvalue of A, with the highest absolute value $\lambda_{\max}$, is smaller than 1. If $\lambda_{\max} > 1$, the grammar is inconsistent; $\lambda_{\max} = 1$ produces various special problems which we will leave out of our discussion.

Let us again consider grammar G of Theorem 3.6., with productions $S \to SS$ and $S \to a$. Let $p(S \to SS) = p$, and $p(S \to a) = 1 - p$. Under what conditions will G be consistent? In this case matrix A has one cell: $A = [2p]$, because S occurs twice to the right of the arrow in the production $S \to SS$ with probability p. The only eigenvalue of A is then $2p$, and the grammar is consequently consistent when $2p < 1$ or $p < \frac{1}{2}$. It is inconsistent if $p > \frac{1}{2}$ (as was the case in the original example where $p = \frac{2}{3}$). In this case the grammar is also consistent when $p = \frac{1}{2}$.

4

FINITE AUTOMATA

In the present chapter we shall regard that which generative systems give as output, as the input of accepting systems. By definition, grammars are finite systems of rules by which potentially infinite sets of sentences can be generated. In this and the following chapters we shall show that for every language-type a mechanism can be constructed which is able to accept precisely the sentences of a language. In other words, given a language L of type-i, an automaton can be devised which can decide, after a finite number of operations, for the sentences of L and for no other string, that a sentence belongs to L. In generating a sentence, a grammar ascribes a structural description to it in passing; in a similar way, when an equivalent automaton accepts a sentence, an equivalent structural description unfolds.

It would, however, be incorrect to conclude from this symmetry that a mechanism finite in size can accept anything which is generated by a finite grammar. Such a mechanism can indeed be of finite description, but in most cases it will have to contain an infinite number of parts. In fact, only one of the language types which we have treated — the class of regular languages — is recognizable through finite means.

In this chapter we shall present a survey of the theory of finite automata, and we shall show (1) that there is a finite recognition-automaton for every regular language, and (2) that for every set of strings which is accepted by a given finite automaton, a regular grammar can be found which generates precisely the same strings. Some special types of finite automata, such as nondeterministic and *k*-limited automata, will also be briefly discussed. In the final paragraph we shall mention some of the properties of probabilistic finite automata.

4.1. DEFINITIONS AND CONCEPTS

A FINITE AUTOMATON, FA, is a system (S, I, δ, s_0, F) in which

(1) S is a finite nonempty set of STATES. At any given moment the automaton must be in one of these states. Individual states are generally denoted by the letters s or t, with subscripts when needed.

(2) I is a finite nonempty (INPUT) VOCABULARY. Its elements ("words") are represented by letters from the beginning of the Latin alphabet. I^* is the set of strings, finite in length, composed of the elements of I, including the null-string λ. Elements of I^* may be represented by letters from the end of the Latin alphabet.

(3) δ is a (STATE) TRANSITION FUNCTION which indicates how the automaton changes states under the influence of an input word. The notation is as follows: $\delta(s, a) = t$ means that the automaton in state s changes to state t at the insertion of word a, where s and t are elements of S. The transformation function is defined for every possible pair of state and input-element: for every $s \in S$ and every $a \in I$, $\delta(s, a)$ is either a state in S, or φ, where φ means that the automaton blocks and no further step is possible. The transition function is also said to MAP the cartesian product $S \times I$ in $S \cup \varphi$. Because $S \times I$ is finite, the transition function consists of a finite set of rules called TRANSITION RULES.

(4) s_0 is a particular element of S, called the INITIAL STATE. It is the state of the automaton when the input process begins.

(5) F is a nonempty set of FINAL STATES in S.

A finite automaton $FA = (S, I, \delta, s_0, F)$ is said to ACCEPT a string $x \in I^*$, if FA, first operating in the initial state s_0, passes through a sequence of states, the last of which is a final state in F, under the influence of the successive elements of x.

Ordinarily the δ-notation is not limited to the input of individual elements of I, but is also used for the input of strings from I^*. If $x = a_1a_2 \ldots a_n$, and FA contains the following transition rules: $\delta(s_1, a_1) = s_2$, $\delta(s_2, a_2) = s_3$, ..., $\delta(s_n, a_n) = s_{n+1}$, where $s_1 = s$ and $s_{n+1} = t$, we may write $\delta(s, x) = t$. Thus $\delta(s, xa) = \delta(\delta(s, x), a)$. By convention $\delta(s, \lambda) = s$. Expanded in this way, the transition function maps $S \times I^*$ in $S \cup \varphi$. We may also say that the automaton ACCEPTS $x \in I^*$ if $\delta(s_o, x) \in F$.

The LANGUAGE T accepted by the finite automaton FA is $\{x|\delta(s_o, x) \in F\}$, the set of strings accepted by the automaton. Such strings are also called SENTENCES.

Two finite automata are EQUIVALENT if they accept the same language.

Finite automata can be pictured as in Figure 4.1. They consist of a CONTROL-UNIT and a READING HEAD along which an INPUT TAPE runs from right to left. A string of input symbols appears on the tape (in the figure $x = a_1a_2 \ldots a_n$). The control-unit can be in only one of a finite number of states at a time. When the reading

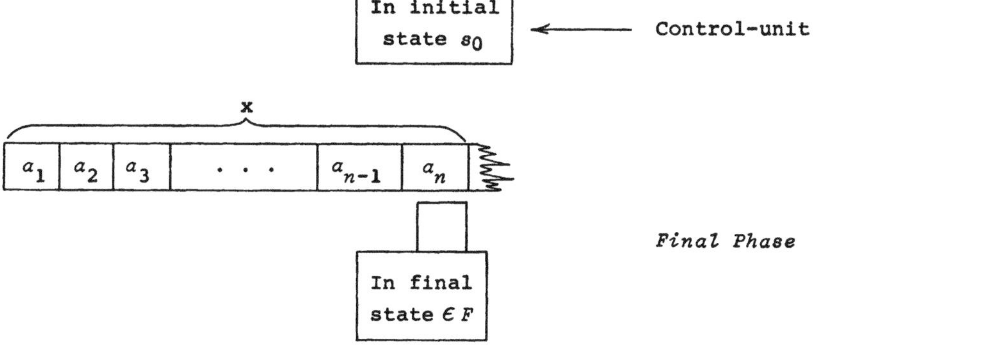

Fig. 4.1. The Accepting of a String $x = a_1a_2 \ldots a_n$ by a Finite Automaton.

head begins to read the first symbol, the control-unit is in the initial state s_0. When the first element (a_1 in the figure) is read, the state of the control-unit can change (according to the transition rule concerned). The tape then moves one space to the left. The next input symbol (a_2 in the figure) is read in the new state, and a second change of state may take place, according to the respective transition rule. The tape again moves one space to the left. This process continues until the control-unit arrives at a final state in F. The string of symbols read up to that point is then said to have been accepted by the automaton. Figure 4.1. shows the initial and final phases.

It is also possible visually to represent what occurs in the control-unit during reading; this is done by means of a TRANSITION-DIAGRAM. We shall illustrate this with a few examples.

EXAMPLE 4.1. Let $FA = (S, I, \delta, s_0, F)$ be a finite automaton with $S = \{s_0, s_1\}$, $I = \{a, b\}$, $F = \{s_1\}$, and where δ contains the following transition rules:

$$\delta(s_0, a) = s_1 \qquad \delta(s_0, b) = \varphi$$
$$\delta(s_1, b) = s_0 \qquad \delta(s_1, a) = \varphi$$

The transition-diagram for this automaton is given in Figure 4.2.

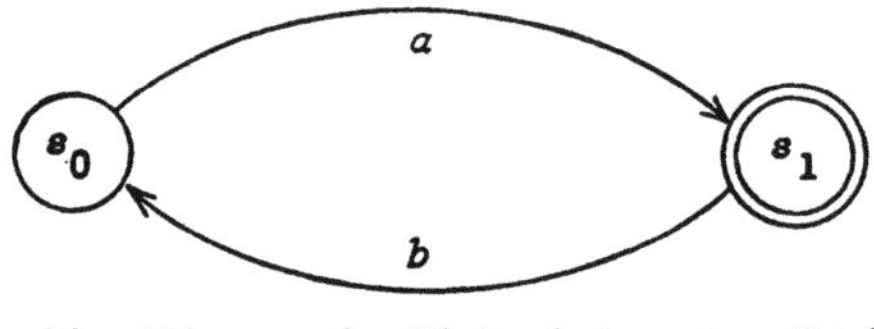

Fig. 4.2. Transition-Diagram for Finite Automaton FA (Example 4.1.).
initial state is s_0
final state (circled twice) is s_1

Such a diagram should be read in the following terms. Every state is shown by means of a circle in which the name of the state is given. For every nonblocking transition rule $\delta(s, a) = t$, there is an arrow in the diagram going from the circle labeled s to the circle labeled t; the input symbol a is written near the arrow. In Figure 4.2. it is clear that the automaton in question has two states, that it passes from state s_0 to state s_1 when a is read, and that it returns from state s_1 to state s_0 when b is read. String a is obviously accepted by this automaton, because beginning in the initial state s_0, it passes to the (only) final state s_1 when a is read. Another way of coming to the final state s_1 is by reading the string aba: the automaton passes successively from s_0 to s_1, then back to s_0, and again to s_1; because s_0 is an initial state and s_1 is a final state, the string aba, by definition, is accepted. This automaton accepts all strings a, aba, $ababa$, ... The language is $T = \{a(ba)^*\}$.

EXAMPLE 4.2. Let $FA = (S, I, \delta, s_0, F)$ be a finite automaton with $S = \{s_0, s_1, s_2\}$, $I = \{a, b, c, d, e, f\}$, $F = \{s_0\}$, and with the following transition rules in δ:

$\delta(s_0, a) = s_1$	$\delta(s_2, e) = s_0$
$\delta(s_1, b) = s_1$	$\delta(s_2, f) = s_0$
$\delta(s_1, c) = s_2$	$\delta\,(-, -) = \varphi$ for all other pairs
$\delta(s_1, d) = s_2$	

The transition-diagram for this automaton is given in Figure 4.3.

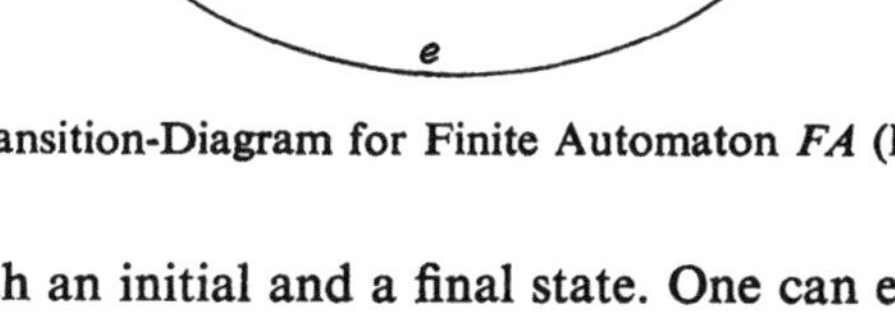

Fig. 4.3. Transition-Diagram for Finite Automaton *FA* (Example 4.2.).

Here s_0 is both an initial and a final state. One can easily see from the diagram that the automaton will accept all strings which bring it from the initial state s_0 back to the final state s_0; these are such strings as *adf*, *ace*, *ade*, *abdf*, *abbce*, etc. Each of these strings is composed of first an a, then a string of 0 or more b's, then either a d or a c ($d \vee c$), and finally either an e or an f ($e \vee f$), thus strings of the form $ab^*(c \vee d)(e \vee f)$. As in the preceding example, however, after returning to the final state s_0, one can make still another turn in the automaton, returning once again to s_0, and continue doing so. The language accepted by this automaton is $T = \{(ab^*(c \vee d)(e \vee f))^*\}$. The machine also accepts λ, because by definition $\delta(s_0, \lambda) = s_0$, bringing the automaton from the initial to the final state.

Beside the fact that initial and final states are identical, this automaton has the peculiarity of allowing LOOPS, by which a state s_1 can be transformed into itself again. Moreover, there are two pairs of EQUIVALENT INITIAL SYMBOLS, d and c, and e and f, which under all circumstances have the same effect on the operation of the automaton.

Instead of a transition-diagram, one can also use a TRANSITION-TABLE to show the structure of an automaton. A transition-table is a matrix in which the row-elements represent the states of an automaton, and the column-elements represent the possible input symbols. Every matrix-element shows a state (or φ) which is reached from a given state (row-element) and a given input symbol (column-element). An example of such a matrix is the following transition-table for finite automaton FA of Example 4.2.

input elements

	a	b	c	d	e	f
s_0	s_1	φ	φ	φ	φ	φ
s_1	φ	s_1	s_2	s_2	φ	φ
s_2	φ	φ	φ	φ	s_0	s_0

Ordinarily the φ is omitted in such a matrix. A transition-table contains precisely the same information as a transition-diagram.

Some finite automata are K-LIMITED. A k-limited automaton is a finite automaton the state of which is determined at every moment by the last k (or fewer) accepted input symbols. The automaton of Example 4.2. is 1-limited. As is clear from the transition-diagram (Figure 4.3.), the automaton, after having accepted a, can be only in state s_1; after accepting b, only in state s_1; after accepting c, only in state s_2; after accepting d, only in state s_2; after accepting e, only in state s_o; and after accepting f, only in state s_o. Likewise in each column of the transition-table, only one state is mentioned.

A 2-limited automaton is shown in Figure 4.4., both in diagrammatic and in tabular form. It is clear that immediately after accepting an a, the machine can be in one of two states, either s_1 or s_2. The automaton is therefore not 1-limited, but 2-limited, for after accepting aa, it is in state s_2; after accepting ab it is in s_o, and after ba, in s_1. It can never accept bb.

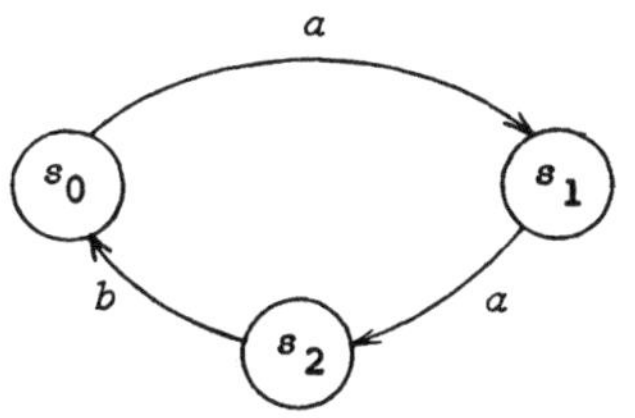

	a	b
s_0	s_1	
s_1	s_2	
s_2		s_0

Fig. 4.4. Transition-Diagram and Transition-Table for a 2-limited Automaton.

Figure 4.5. shows that not all finite automata are k-limited; it represents an automaton which is k-limited for no finite k. Even when this automaton has accepted an arbitrarily long string of b's, we do not know if it is in state s_o or in state s_1.

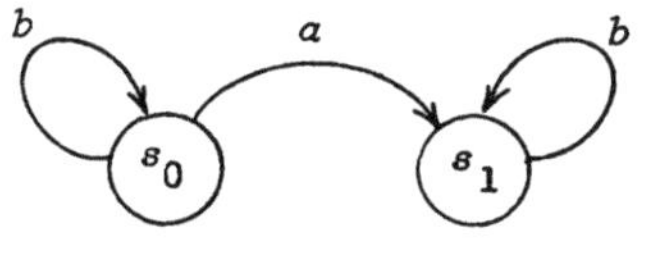

	a	b
s_0	s_1	s_0
s_1		s_1

Fig. 4.5. Transition-Diagram and Transition-Table for an Automaton which is k-limited for no Finite k.

If s_o is the initial state and s_1 the final state, then the language which the automaton accepts is $T = \{b^*ab^*\}$. The k-limited automaton is of some interest in dealing with Markov processes (cf. Volume II, 6.1., and Volume III, 3.2.).

4.2. NONDETERMINISTIC FINITE AUTOMATA

The finite automaton defined in the preceding paragraph has the property that for every state and input symbol, the state which follows (or φ) is unambiguously determined. Such an automaton is therefore called a DETERMINISTIC automaton. But, for two reasons, it remains necessary to define the nondeterministic variant of finite automata here. The first reason is that such a definition will allow us more easily to establish the relationship between finite automata and regular grammars. The second reason is that the probabilistic automaton (cf. paragraph 4.4.) is in turn a generalization of the finite automaton.

A NONDETERMINISTIC FINITE AUTOMATON *NFA* is a system (S, I, δ, s_0, F) which is in every way equal to a deterministic finite automaton, except for the transition rules δ. The transition rules of a nondeterministic finite automaton have the following form: $\delta(s, a) = \{t_1, t_2, \ldots, t_k\} = D$, where $0 \leqslant k < \infty$; s, $t_i \in S$, and $D \subset S$. In other words, for every pair of state and input symbols, there is a finite set of states at which the automaton can arrive. δ is said to be a mapping of $S \times I$ in the subset of S (where φ is the empty subset). A deterministic finite automaton is actually a particular case of nondeterministic finite automata: it covers those cases where for all transition rules $k = 1$ or $k = 0$.

When can one say that $x \in I^*$ is accepted by a nondeterministic finite automaton? Suppose that $x = a_1a_2 \ldots a_n$, and that the finite automaton *FA* contains the following transition rules: $\delta(s_0, a_1) = D_1$, $s_1 \in D_1$; $\delta(s_1, a_2) = D_2$, $s_2 \in D_2$; ...; $\delta(s_{n-1}, a_n) = D_n$, $s_n \in D_n$ and $s_n \in F$, then x is said to be accepted by the automaton. Thus, if there is some succession of states allowed by the transition rules, according to which x brings the automaton from s_0 to a final state, the nondeterministic finite automaton is said to accept x.

The operation of a nondeterministic finite automaton is also easy to represent by way of a transition diagram, as becomes apparent in the following example.

EXAMPLE 4.3. Let $NFA = (S, I, \delta, s_o, F)$ be a nondeterministic finite automaton where $s = \{s_o, s_1, s_2\}$, $I = \{a, b\}$, $F = \{s_2\}$, and δ contains the following transition rules:

$\delta(s_o, a) = \{s_o, s_1\}$
$\delta(s_1, a) = \{s_2\}$
$\delta(s_1, b) = \{s_1, s_2\}$
$\delta\ (-, -) =$ for all other pairs.

Figure 4.6. shows the transition-diagram for this automaton. Among the strings which can bring the automaton from the initial state s_o to the final state s_2 are the following: *aa*, *ab*, *aaa*, *aab*, *aba*, *abb*, and so forth. In general, the language accepted by this automaton is $T = \{a^*ab^*(a \vee b)\}$.

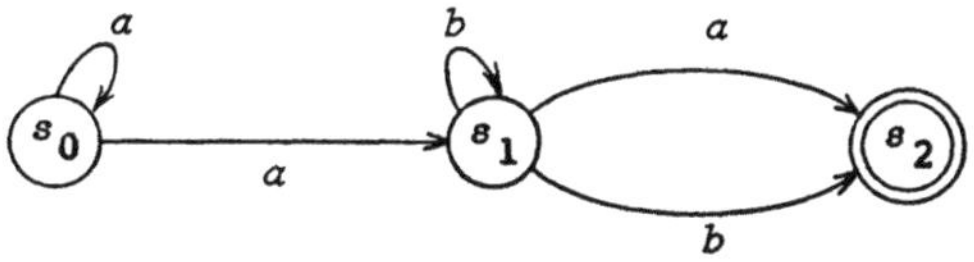

Fig. 4.6. Transition-Diagram for the Nondeterministic Finite Automaton *NFA* (Example 4.3.). The final state s_2 is circled twice.

The following important theorem is valid for nondeterministic finite automata.

THEOREM 4.1. For every nondeterministic finite automaton there exists an equivalent deterministic finite automaton.

The proof of this theorem, for which we refer the reader to Rabin and Scott (1959), will be briefly discussed later. We shall first illustrate it by returning to Example 4.3. We can construct a finite automaton *FA* equivalent to the nondeterministic finite automaton

NFA of that example in the following way. *NFA* had three states, i.e. $S = \{s_o, s_1, s_2\}$; the corresponding *FA* will have seven states, namely, $[s_o]$, $[s_1]$, $[s_2]$, $[s_o, s_1]$, $[s_o, s_2]$, $[s_1, s_2]$, and $[s_o, s_1, s_2]$. These states are thus called after all possible nonempty subsets of S. We maintain the input vocabulary, and in order to establish the new set of transition rules we proceed as follows. Let us begin with $\delta'([s_o], a)$. In *NFA* $\delta(s_o, a) = \{s_o, s_1\}$; in *FA* let $\delta'([s_o], a) = [s_o, s_1]$. Notice that this latter is one state and not two. Further let $\delta'([s_1], a) = [s_2]$ because $\delta(s_1, a) = \{s_2\}$, and $\delta'([s_2], a) = \varphi$ because $\delta(s_2, a) = \varphi$. For $\delta'([s_o, s_1], a)$ we proceed as follows. In *NFA* $\delta(s_o, a) = \{s_o, s_1\}$ and $\delta(s_1, a) = \{s_2\}$. The union of $\delta(s_o, a)$ and $\delta(s_1, a)$ is thus $\{s_o, s_1, s_2\}$, and in *FA* we let $\delta'([s_o, s_1], a) = [s_o, s_1, s_2]$. Again the latter is a single state. Similarly we construct $\delta'([s_o, s_2], a) = [s_o, s_1]$, etc. This procedure leads to the establishment of the following list of transition rules:

$\delta'([s_o], a) = [s_o, s_1]$	$\delta'([s_o, s_2], a) = [s_o, s_1]$
$\delta'([s_1], a) = [s_2]$	$\delta'([s_1, s_2], a) = [s_2]$
$\delta'([s_1], b) = [s_1, s_2]$	$\delta'([s_1, s_2], b) = [s_1, s_2]$
$\delta'([s_o, s_1], a) = [s_o, s_1, s_2]$	$\delta'([s_o, s_1, s_2], a) = [s_o, s_1, s_2]$
$\delta'([s_o, s_1], b) = [s_1, s_2]$	$\delta'([s_o, s_1, s_2], b) = [s_1, s_2]$

For all other δ' (—, —), δ' (—, —) $= \varphi$.

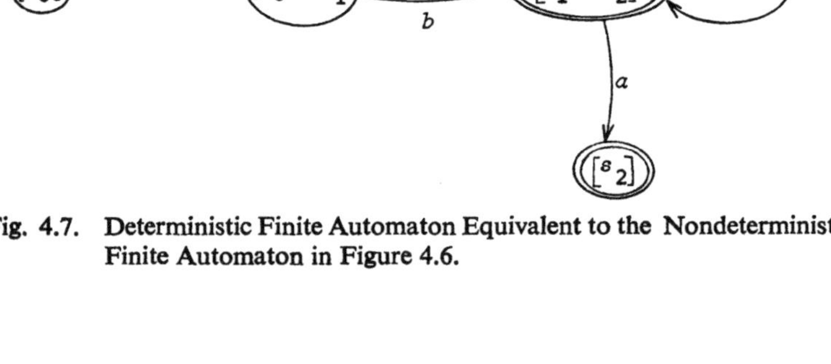

Fig. 4.7. Deterministic Finite Automaton Equivalent to the Nondeterministic Finite Automaton in Figure 4.6.

The set of final states F' in FA is defined as consisting of those states in which the label of a final state of NFA occurs. The only final state in NFA is s_2, and therefore $F' = \{[s_2], [s_o, s_2], [s_1, s_2], [s_o, s_1, s_2]\}$. Finally we take $[s_o]$ as the initial state in FA, and we affirm that FA is equivalent to NFA.

The transition-diagram for FA is given in Figure 4.7. The final states in the diagram are circled twice. The reader should notice that states $[s_1]$ and $[s_o, s_2]$ do not appear in the figure; this is because neither of them serves as the output of any transition rule. They are superfluous and consequently omitted. The diagram shows that FA accepts precisely the language $\{a^*ab^*(a \vee b)\}$.

PROOF OF THEOREM 4.1. (résumé). The proof follows the construction which we have just described. The states of FA correspond to the nonempty subsets of S in NFA. The transition rules are constructed as we have shown, and the set of final states F' in FA consists of those states which have one or more elements of F in their labels. By induction on the length of the string of input symbols it can be shown that FA is equivalent to NFA.

Because, inversely, deterministic finite automata are special cases of nondeterministic finite automata, we can conclude that the class of finite automata is equivalent to the class of nondeterministic finite automata; they accept the same class of languages.

4.3. FINITE AUTOMATA AND REGULAR GRAMMARS

In this paragraph we shall give proof of the equivalence of finite automata and regular grammars. The languages accepted by finite automata are exactly the same as those generated by regular grammars, and vice versa.

THEOREM 4.2. For every finite automaton FA there exists a regular grammar G such that $T(FA) = L(G)$.

PROOF. Let $FA = (S, I, \delta, s_o, F)$ be a finite automaton. We must construct a regular grammar $G = (V_N, V_T, P, S)$ such that

(i) $V_N = S$
(ii) $V_T = I$
(iii) $S = s_o$
(iv) $A \to aB$ is in P as $\delta(A, a) = B$
$A \to a$ is in P as $\delta(A, a) = C$, where $C \in F$
(notice that B and C are used here as labels for states)

We shall now show that G is equivalent to FA. For this, two conditions must be fulfilled: (1) If $x \in T(FA)$, then $x \in L(G)$, and (2) if $x \in L(G)$, then $x \in T(FA)$.

(1) $x \in T(FA)$. If this is so, then by definition $\delta(s_o, x)$ in F. We write x as $a_1a_2 \dots a_n$. We presuppose that $\lambda \notin T(FA)$, and that therefore $n > 0$. In that case $\delta(s_o, x) = \delta(\delta(s_o, a_1a_2 \dots a_{n-1}), a_n)$ (cf. paragraph 4.1. (5)), and continuing in the same way $\delta(s_o, x) = \delta(\delta(\dots (s_o, a_1), a_2), \dots), a_n)$. Because $\delta(s_o, x)$ in F, there is a sequence of states $s_o, s_1, \dots, s_n$ ($s_i \in S$; s_i and s_j are not necessarily different) such that $\delta(s_o, a_1) = s_1$, $\delta(s_1, a_2) = \delta(\delta(s_o, a_1), a_2) = s_2$, ..., $\delta(s_{n-1}, a_n) = s_n$, where $s_n \in F$. But then there are also productions $S = s_o \to a_1s_1$, $s_1 \to a_2s_2$, ..., $s_{n-1} \to a_n$ in P, on the basis of the construction of G. It is then clear that $S \overset{*}{\Rightarrow} a_1a_2 \dots a_n = x$.

(2) $x \in L(G)$. By definition $S \overset{*}{\Rightarrow} x$. Let x be written as $a_1a_2 \dots a_n$. Then there are productions $S = s_o \to a_1s_1$, $s_1 \to a_2s_2$, ..., $s_{n-2} \to a_{n-1}s_{n-1}$ and $s_{n-1} \to a_n$ in P for certain s_i in V_N. But that means that FA contains the following transition rules: $\delta(s_o, a_1) = s_1$, $\delta(s_1, a_2) = s_2$, ..., $\delta(s_{n-2}, a_{n-1}) = s_{n-1}$, $\delta(s_{n-1}, a_n) = s_n$ with s_n in F (this follows from the definition of G). It is evident that with these transition rules FA accepts the string $a_1a_2 \dots a_n = x$.

It follows from (1) and (2) that FA and G are equivalent for sentences of length > 0. If FA also accepts λ, the theorem holds only if we maintain the convention of paragraph 2.1., i.e. that by definition G also generates λ.

EXAMPLE 4.4. Let us construct a grammar equivalent to the finite automaton FA in Example 4.1. We recall that $FA = (S, I, \delta, s_o, F)$, where $S = \{s_o, s_1\}$, $I = \{a, b\}$, $F = \{s_1\}$, and with the following transition rules: $\delta(s_0, a) = s_1$ and $\delta(s_1, b) = s_0$ (for all other pairs $\delta(-, -) = \varphi$).

The construction as shown in the proof is as follows: $G = (V_N, V_T, P, S)$, with $V_N = \{s_0 = S, s_1\}$, $V_T = \{a, b\}$, and $P = \{s_0 \to as_1, s_0 \to a, s_1 \to bs_0\}$. Notice that on the basis of (iv), the transition rule $\delta(s_0, a) = s_1$ leads to two productions in G: $s_0 \to as_1$ and $s_0 \to a$.

THEOREM 4.3. For every regular grammar G there exists a finite automaton FA such that $T(FA) = L(G)$.

PROOF. We shall prove that a nondeterministic finite automaton NFA can be found so that $T(NFA) = L(G)$. The theorem is then valid because for every nondeterministic finite automaton NFA there exists an equivalent finite automaton FA (Theorem 4.1.).

Let $G = (V_N, V_T, P, S)$ be a regular grammar. We construct $NFA = (S, I, \delta, s_0, F)$ as follows:

(i) $S = V_N \cup X$
(ii) $I = V_T$
(iii) $\delta(A, a)$ contains X (*inter alia*) if $A \to a$ in P
$\delta(A, a)$ contains every B for which $A \to aB$ in P
$\delta(X, a) = \varphi$ for every a in V_T
(iv) $s_0 = S$
(v) $F = \{X\}$, if $\lambda \notin L(G)$; $F = \{X, S\}$, if $\lambda \in L(G)$

Once again the proof of equivalence takes place in two steps. First it must be shown that if $x \in L(G)$, where $x = a_1a_2 \dots a_n$, then $x \in T(NFA)$. Afterward the inverse must be shown.

(1) $x \in L(G)$. If $x \in L(G)$ and $|x| > 0$, then there is a derivation $S \Rightarrow a_1A_1 \Rightarrow \dots \Rightarrow a_1a_2 \dots a_{n-1}A_{n-1} \Rightarrow a_1a_2 \dots a_n$ for some sequence $A_1, \dots, A_{n-1}$ of variables in V_N. P thus contains the productions $S \to a_1A_1$, $A_1 \to a_2A_2$, ... $A_{n-1} \to a_n$. It appears, then, from the construction of NFA that $A_1 \in \delta(S, a_1)$, $A_2 \in \delta(A_1, a_2)$, ... $X \in \delta(A_{n-1}, a_n)$. But if the transition rules are valid, $x = a_1a_2 \dots a_n$ is in $T(NFA)$. If $\lambda \in L(G)$, then $S \in F$ (see (v)), and because $\delta(S, \lambda)$ contains S by definition, $\lambda \in T(NFA)$.

(2) $x \in T(NFA)$. If $|x| > 0$ and x is accepted by NFA, then there are states S, A_1, ..., A_{n-1}, X, where $A_1 \in \delta(S, a_1)$, $A_2 \in \delta(A_1, a_2)$, ..., $X \in \delta(A_{n-1}, a_n)$. But from the construction of NFA it appears that P must also have productions $S \to a_1A_1$, ..., $A_{n-1} \to a_n$. It follows from this that $S \overset{*}{\Rightarrow} a_1a_2 \ldots a_n = x$. If $\lambda \in T(NFA)$, then $S \in F$. But $S \in F$ only if $\lambda \in L(G)$ (see (v)).

The equivalence of G and NFA follows from arguments (1) and (2). It follows from Theorem 4.1. that there must also exist an FA equivalent to G.

EXAMPLE 4.5. Let us construct a nondeterministic finite automaton NFA which accepts the language generated by regular grammar G in Example 2.1. We recall that $G = (V_N, V_T, P, S)$ where $V_N = \{S, B\}$, $V_T = \{a, b\}$, and $P = \{S \to aB,\ B \to bS,\ B \to b\}$, and that $L(G) = \{(ab)^*\}$. We shall now construct $NFA = (S, I, \delta, s_0, F)$ according to the procedure given in the proof. Thus $S = \{S, B, X\}$, $I = \{a, b\}$, δ contains the following transition rules: $\delta(S, a) = \{B\}$, $\delta(B, b) = \{X, S\}$, $\delta\,(-, -) = \varphi$ for all other pairs; finally, $F = \{X, S\}$. The transition-diagram for automaton NFA is given in Figure 4.8.

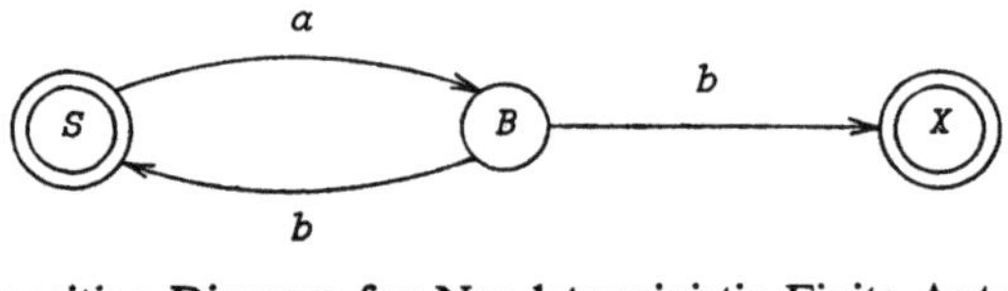

Fig. 4.8. Transition-Diagram for Nondeterministic Finite Automaton NFA which accepts language $\{(ab)^*\}$.

Together Theorems 4.2. and 4.3. show the equivalence of finite automata and regular grammars. We can employ this equivalence in order to prove certain theorems concerning regular grammars by means of theorems concerning finite automata, and vice-versa. Theorem 2.5. is a good example of this.

THEOREM 2.5. The product of two regular languages is regular.

PROOF. Let L_1 and L_2 be regular languages; let L_3 consist of the strings xy where $x \in L_1$ and $y \in L_2$. There is a regular grammar for L_1, and therefore we know, on the basis of the equivalency theorem, that there is also a finite automaton which accepts L_1. We shall call this finite automaton $FA_1 = (S, I_1, \delta_1, s_o, F_1)$. Likewise there is a finite automaton $FA_2 = (T, I_2, \delta_2, t_o, F_2)$ which precisely accepts L_2. F_1 and F_2 can always be chosen such that they have no states in common. We must now construct a nondeterministic finite automaton $NFA = (U, I_3, \delta_3, u_o, F_3)$, which, in a way, connects FA_1 and FA_2 "in series". We define NFA as follows:

(i) $U = S \cup T$

(ii) $I_3 = I_1 \cup I_2$

(iii) $\delta_3(u, a) = \{\delta_1(s, a)\}$ for every s in $S - F_1$. In this way NFA can begin with a given input as if it were FA_1.

$\delta_3(u, a) = \{\delta_1(s, a), \delta_2(t_o, a)\}$ for every s in F_1. If NFA arrives at a final state of FA_1, it can freely (nondeterministically) either continue to another state of FA_1 (if this is also possible for FA_1) or pass on to FA_2. This latter is possible only when NFA has already reached a final state of F_1 (the transition rule is applicable only if s is in F_1) and when a can be the first symbol of a sentence of L_2 (notice that the initial state of FA_2 is t_o).
$\delta_3(u, a) = \{\delta_2(t, a)\}$ for every t in T. This guarantees that once NFA has "transferred" to FA_2 it will continue to operate as FA_2.

(iv) $u_o = s_o$

(v) $F_3 = F_2$ if $\lambda \notin L_2$. This guarantees that NFA accepts the input when the end of a sentence of L_2 is reached.
$F_3 = F_1 \cup F_2$ if $\lambda \in L_2$. If FA_2 accepts the null-string, it accepts all sentences $x\lambda = x$, i.e. the sentences of L_1. The automaton must be able to accept in each of the final states of F_1.

The construction of NFA guarantees that it will accept precisely the sentences $xy \in L_3$. But, on the basis of Theorem 4.1., there is also a deterministic finite automaton FA which does the same.

It follows from Theorem 4.2. that there is a regular grammar for L_3, and that L_3 is consequently regular.

The reader may now himself prove the lemma which was used at the proof of Theorem 2.8., with the help of finite automata.[1]

4.4. PROBABILISTIC FINITE AUTOMATA

We shall mention probabilistic automata only in the present paragraph. It is only on the subject of probabilistic finite automata that literature of any considerable size is available.

The probabilistic finite automaton (*PFA*) is a generalization of the nondeterministic finite automaton; a probability is assigned to every possible transition. Before presenting a formal definition of probabilistic finite automata, we shall discuss the manner, step by step, in which the generalization is made.

If it is true for a nondeterministic finite automaton *NFA* that $\delta(s, a) = \{s_1, s_2, \ldots, s_n\}$, we can define $p_i(s, a)$ for a probabilistic finite automaton *PFA* as the chance that the automaton will pass from state s to state s_i, given the input symbol a. We shall suppose that every probabilistic finite automaton is normalized, i.e. $\sum_{i=1}^{n} p_i(s, a) = 1$. In other words, the total chance for a state transition under the influence of a given input is 1. We shall return to the merits of this convention at the end of this paragraph. There is no reason why the chance for transition to a particular state could not be zero. In general we shall suppose that $1 \geqslant p_i(s, a) \geqslant 0$. Because transitions which cannot take place in a nondeterministic finite automaton can in a probabilistic finite automaton be considered as transitions where $p = 0$, we may give a more general definition of the transition function δ in a probabilistic finite automaton. If such an automaton *PFA* has n states, then $\delta(s, a)$ can

[1] To do so one should construct a nondeterministic finite automaton *NFA* which normally operates as FA_1 (which accepts L_1) except with transitions $\delta(s, a)$ where a is the critical terminal element. In such cases FA_2 (which accepts L_2) should be made to "take over" until a state in F_2 is reached. This should then act as $\delta(s, a)$, in order for *NFA* to be able to go on functioning as FA_1.

unambiguously be regarded as a row (vector) $(p_1, p_2, \ldots, p_n)$, where $p_i = p_i(s, a)$. For impossible transitions $p_i = 0$; for all other transitions p_i is the transition probability. Thus for every pair (s, a) where $s \in S$ and $a \in I$, δ is a vector of n numbers. If, for an element a, we wish to represent all the vectors, we can show them in matrix form as follows:

$$\begin{array}{c|ccccccc} & s_1 & s_2 & \ldots & s_j & \ldots & s_n \\ \hline \delta(s_1, a) & P_{11} & P_{12} & \ldots & P_{1j} & \ldots & P_{1n} \\ \delta(s_2, a) & P_{21} & P_{22} & \ldots & P_{2j} & \ldots & P_{2n} \\ & \vdots & \vdots & & \vdots & & \vdots \\ \delta(s_i, a) & P_{i1} & P_{i2} & \ldots & P_{ij} & \ldots & P_{in} \\ & \vdots & \vdots & & \vdots & & \vdots \\ \delta(s_n, a) & P_{n1} & P_{n2} & \ldots & P_{nj} & \ldots & P_{nn} \end{array}$$

For the sake of brevity we shall call this entire matrix $M(a)$, the TRANSITION-MATRIX for element a. Matrix-element p_{ij} in $M(a)$ means that if the automaton is in state s_i and reads the input symbol a, there is a chance of p_{ij} that a transition to state s_j will take place. Normalization guarantees that the sum of the elements in a row in this matrix is equal to 1. The matrix is square $(n \times n)$, and is thus a stochastic matrix.

To include all the transition rules in *PFA* we would have to compose similar matrices for each of the input elements. If $I = \{a_1, a_2, \ldots, a_m\}$, we define M as the set of transition-matrices for the elements of I. Thus $M = \{M(a_1), M(a_2), \ldots, M(a_m)\}$.

Finally, we wish to open the possibility that the initial state of *PFA* is also random. For each of the n states we must define an INITIAL PROBABILITY $p(s)$, which represents the chance that at the first input the automaton is in state s. Since we wish *PFA* with certainty to be initially in one of the n states, we let $\sum_{i=1}^{n} p(s_i) = 1$. One can now no longer speak of an initial state, but rather of an INITIAL DISTRIBUTION; this simply means the string of initial probabilities $(p(s_1), p(s_2), \ldots, p(s_n))$. This vector is denoted by s_0.

At this point we can define a probabilistic finite automaton.

A PROBABILISTIC FINITE AUTOMATON is a system $PFA = (S, I,$

M, s_0, F), in which S is a finite set of states, I is a finite input vocabulary, M is the set of transition-matrices, s_0 is the initial distribution and $F \subset S$ is the set of final states.

EXAMPLE 4.6. Take the probabilistic finite automaton $PFA = (\{s_1, s_2\}, \{a, b\}, \{M(a), M(b)\}, (1, 0), \{s_2\})$ with $M(a) = \begin{bmatrix} 0 & 1 \\ 0 & 1 \end{bmatrix}$ and $M(b) = \begin{bmatrix} \frac{2}{3} & \frac{1}{3} \\ \frac{1}{3} & \frac{2}{3} \end{bmatrix}$. PFA has two states and the chance of starting in s_1 is 1 (because $s_0 = (1,0)$). From transition-matrix $M(a)$ we learn that when the automaton is in state s_1 and reads the input symbol a, it has a chance of 1 to change to state s_2; if in state s_2 input of a leads with probability 1 to transition to s_2, i.e. PFA remains in s_2. Transition-matrix $M(b)$ shows what happens when the input is the symbol b. Once again all this is better shown by a transition-diagram. In a transition-diagram for a probabilistic finite automaton, the various arrows are labelled not only with the respective input elements, but also with the corresponding transition probabilities. Figure 4.9. gives the diagram for the automaton in this example. Arrows for transitions the probabilities of which are equal to 0 have been omitted.

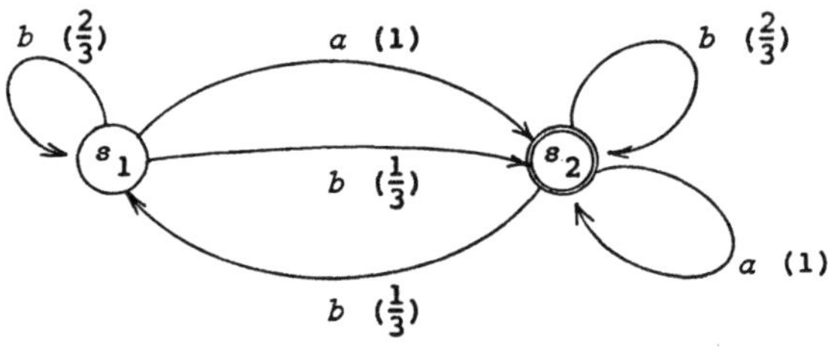

Fig. 4.9. Transition-Diagram for a Probabilistic Finite Automaton (Example 4.6.).

The diagram shows that starting in state s_1 the automaton has a chance of 1 to pass to final state s_2 when the input symbol a is read; this chance becomes $\frac{1}{3}$ when the input symbol is b. What will be the chance for the transition if the input is the string ab?

The element a brings the automaton, with a probability of 1, to state s_2; the element b will maintain the automaton in state s_2 with a probability of $\frac{2}{3}$. If the transitions are independent of each other (which is our presupposition here), the string ab brings the automaton to state s_2 with a probability of $1 \cdot \frac{2}{3} = \frac{2}{3}$. What then will be the chance that the string ab will bring the automaton back to state s_1? Obviously this will be $1 \cdot \frac{1}{3} = \frac{1}{3}$. Likewise the string ab will take the automaton from state s_2 back to state s_2 with the probability $1 \cdot \frac{2}{3} = \frac{2}{3}$, and from state s_1 back to state s_1 with probability $1 \cdot \frac{1}{3} = \frac{1}{3}$. In this way we have in fact found a transition-matrix for the string ab:

$$M(ab) = \begin{bmatrix} \frac{1}{3} & \frac{2}{3} \\ \frac{1}{3} & \frac{2}{3} \end{bmatrix}.$$

It is also quite easy to see that $M(ab)$ is the matrix product of $M(a)$ and $M(b)$:

$$M(ab) = \begin{bmatrix} 0 & 1 \\ 0 & 1 \end{bmatrix} \cdot \begin{bmatrix} \frac{2}{3} & \frac{1}{3} \\ \frac{1}{3} & \frac{2}{3} \end{bmatrix} = \begin{bmatrix} \frac{1}{3} & \frac{2}{3} \\ \frac{1}{3} & \frac{2}{3} \end{bmatrix}.$$

In general we can define the TRANSITION-MATRIX $M(x)$ FOR A STRING $x = a_1a_2 \ldots a_n$ as the product $M(x) = M(a_1) \cdot M(a_2) \cdot \ldots \cdot M(a_n)$. In such a matrix one can read, for all pairs s_i, s_j, the probability that the entry of an input x will cause the probabilistic finite automaton to change from state s_i to state s_j.

For the interested reader we can likewise easily indicate, in matrix notation, the chance that a final state be reached at all with a given string, given vector s_o, the string of initial probabilities. For this purpose, we define a FINAL VECTOR s_f as a string of n numbers, analogous to s_o, corresponding to the n states in S and in the same order. For every state, the corresponding number is 1 if the state is a final state, and 0 when this is not the case. Thus $s_f = (q_1, q_2, \ldots, q_n)$ where $q_i = 1$ if $s_i \in F$, and $q_i = 0$ if $s_i \notin F$. The final vector in Example 4.6. is thus (0, 1), for only s_2 is a final state. The chance that x will bring the automaton to a final state is given in matrix notation as $s_o M(x)\, s'_f$.[1] Thus the chance that the string *ab* will bring the automaton of Example 4.6. to a final state is equal to

$$(1, 0) \cdot \begin{bmatrix} \frac{1}{3} & \frac{2}{3} \\ \frac{1}{3} & \frac{2}{3} \end{bmatrix} \cdot \begin{bmatrix} 0 \\ 1 \end{bmatrix} = (\tfrac{1}{3} \cdot \tfrac{2}{3}) \cdot \begin{bmatrix} 0 \\ 1 \end{bmatrix} = \tfrac{2}{3}.$$

With these means at our disposition, we are able to define the language which is accepted by a probabilistic finite automaton. We should like to define that language as the set of strings by which the automaton reaches a final state with a certain minimum probability. What that minimum probability precisely is remains quite arbitrary. We can call it the CUT-POINT PROBABILITY, η.

The η-STOCHASTIC LANGUAGE $T(PFA, \eta)$ is the set of strings which bring the probabilistic finite automaton *PFA* to a final state with a probability $> \eta$. Formally stated, $T(PFA, \eta) = \{x | s_o M(x) s'_f > \eta\}$.

If $\eta = 0$, the situation is simple; every sentence by which a final state can be reached belongs to *T*. But stricter conditions can be posed. The opposite extreme is $\eta = 1$. However, the chance is never greater than 1 that a sentence will bring the automaton to a final state, and thus $T(PFA, 1)$ is empty for every *PFA*.

THEOREM 4.4. A regular language is η-stochastic for $0 \leqslant \eta < 1$.

PROOF. Let *L* be a regular language, and *FA*, a finite automaton, where $T(FA) = L$. We begin to construct probabilistic finite automaton *PFA* by borrowing *I* and *F* from *FA*. The set of states S' in *PFA* will be $S \cup s_\varphi$, where s_φ is a "dummy" state. A transition-matrix is composed for every $a \in I$ in *PFA* as follows: $p_{ij} = 1$ if $\delta(s_i, a) = s_j$; $p_{ij} = 0$ if $\delta(s_i, a) \neq s_j$, for every pair s_i, s_j in *S*. We let $p_{i\varphi} = 1$ if $\delta(s_i, a) = \varphi$, and $p_{i\varphi} = 0$ in all other cases, for $s_i \in S$. Finally, we let $P_{\varphi\varphi} = 1$, and $p_{\varphi i} = 0$ for every $s_i \in S$. In this way every matrix $M(a)$ is stochastic, and for every sentence *x* in $T(FA)$

[1] s'_f is the TRANSPOSITION of the row-vector, i.e. the row-vector is set up vertically like a column, with the leftmost element at the top. Notice that the definition of a transition-matrix for *x* supposes the stochastic independance of the transitions.

there is a probability of 1 that x will be accepted by PFA, while a final state will be reached with no other string. Because for every sentence s in L, the probability $p(s) = 1$ in $T(PFA)$, it is true for every $0 \leqslant \eta < 1$ that $T(PFA, \eta) = L$.

The inverse of Theorem 4.4. does not hold, but the following theorem is valid.

THEOREM 4.5. Every 0-stochastic language is regular.

PROOF. Let $PFA = (S, I, M, s_0, F)$ be the probabilistic finite automaton which accepts the 0-stochastic language T. We must first construct a nondeterministic finite automaton $NFA(i)$ for a state s_i with initial probability in PFA: $p(s_i) > 0$. We make $NFA(i)$ such that it accepts every sentence which bring PFA from state s_i to a final state, with probability > 0. For this purpose we let the initial state of $NFA(i)$ be s_i, F be the set of final states in $NFA(i)$, and s_l in $\delta(s_j, a_k)$ if the element p_{jl} is greater than 0 in the transition-matrix $M(a_k)$. The language T_i accepted by $NFA(i)$ is regular (Theorems 4.1. and 4.2.).

If we construct a $NFA(i)$ for every s_i in S for which $p(s_i) > 0$, it follows that every sentence which is accepted by PFA, with probability greater than 0, will also be accepted by at least one of the NFA, and that every sentence accepted by one of the NFA will also be accepted by PFA with probability greater than 0. We conclude that the union of all the languages T_i is also regular (Theorem 2.5.).

We close this paragraph with a remark on normalization as used with probabilistic finite automata. The basis for normalization $\sum_{i=1}^{n} p_i(s, a) = 1$ is the input symbol: each input symbol leads to a transition with a probability of 1. The consequence of this normalization is that it is not generally valid that the sentence probabilities in a stochastic language add up to 1. In the degenerate case, for example, where the matrix contains only 1's and 0's, every sentence of the language has a probability of 1, while the language can indeed contain more than one sentence. There is therefore no simple relationship between probabilistic finite automata and regular probabilistic grammars which are normalized on the basis of a nonterminal element. As we have seen, in that case a normalized probabilistic language is generated. Probabilistic finite automata can, of course, also be normalized on another basis, namely the state. In that case the total chance for transition from a given state, taken over all inputs, is equal to 1, thus $\sum_i \sum_j p_i(s, a_j) = 1$. It then becomes possible to show equivalences to probabilistic grammars.

5

PUSH-DOWN AUTOMATA

In the preceding chapter we showed that regular languages can be accepted by finite automata. For languages of a higher order we shall have to refer to systems which are, in some way, infinite in size. To clarify the notion, let us consider a digital computer.

A digital computer is a finite automaton because it has a finite number of parts — for instance, n (including storage) — each of which can be in a finite number of states — let us say k at most. The machine will therefore have no more than k^n states, a finite number. Consequently a computer can accept, in principle, only regular languages; it cannot accept context-free or higher order languages.

One may wonder if there is any practical interest in studying automata which can accept higher order languages, since, in principle, they can never be built. However, the theoretical infiniteness of such automata is of little consequence in practice. The value of n for a sizable computer can easily reach 10^6, and if k is equal to 2, k^n is an astronomically high number. For practical purposes, then, a computer is of unlimited size. It can, within limits which in practice are never reached, accept higher order languages. Most computer languages, such as ALGOL, are in fact context-free or higher order languages.

In this chapter we will discuss one simple infinite automaton, the PUSH-DOWN AUTOMATON. This automaton is infinite because its store, the PUSH-DOWN STORE, is of unlimited capacity. In all other respects it is a finite automaton. We shall show that push-down automata are equivalent to context-free grammars.

5.1. DEFINITIONS AND CONCEPTS

A push-down automaton is a finite automaton to which an unlimited push-down store has been added. A push-down store is somewhat comparable to a narrow knapsack. Imagine that a hiker has placed his matches at the very bottom of his knapsack, then put in his jacket and other articles of clothing, and finally a can of soup, a can opener, and cooking utensils. When the hiker becomes hungry and reaches a brook, he may wish to eat the soup. He removes the cooking utensils, can opener, and the can of soup; this poses no problems, as the last articles placed in the sack are the first to come out. Also, he can add water from the brook. But if he wishes to light a fire to warm the soup, he must first remove the clothing and jacket before he is able to reach the matches: the first things placed in the sack are the last to come out.

We can make an analogy between the hiker and a push-down automaton: the knapsack can be compared to the push-down store (with the matches as the start element), the water and firewood to inputs, and warmth and satisfaction for hunger to state transitions.

The formal definition of a push-down automaton is as follows. A PUSH-DOWN AUTOMATON PDA is a system $(S, I, \Gamma, \delta, s_0, \gamma_0)$ where:

(1) S is a finite nonempty set of STATES, with $s_0 \in S$ as INITIAL STATE.

(2) I is a finite (INPUT) VOCABULARY.

(3) Γ is a finite PUSH-DOWN VOCABULARY, with $\gamma_0 \in \Gamma$ as push-down START SYMBOL, the only element in the store when input begins. Other push-down symbols are $\gamma_1, \gamma_2, \ldots$. The set of finite strings of push-down symbols is Γ^*. Elements of Γ^* are represented by lower case letters from the end of the Greek alphabet, such as χ, ψ, ω. The topmost symbol which at a given moment is found in the push-down store is called the TOP SYMBOL.

(4) δ is the set of TRANSITION RULES. Each rule indicates what will occur when, at a given state, with a given top symbol, a given input symbol (possibly also λ) is introduced, i.e. it shows what the following state will be and by what the top symbol will be replaced. The top symbol may be replaced by (a) an element of Γ;

(b) itself — a special case of (a), the content of the store remains unchanged; (c) an element of Γ^*, thus, a STRING of symbols replaces the top symbol; or (d) the null-string λ — a special case of (c), this amounts to simply removing the top symbol. The notation for these cases is as follows:

(a) $\delta(s_i, a, \gamma_k) = (s_j, \gamma_1)$, where s_i and s_j are states in S, a is an input symbol in I, and γ_k and γ_1 are push-down symbols in Γ.
(b) $\delta(s_i, a, \gamma_k) = (s_j, \gamma_k)$
(c) $\delta(s_i, a, \gamma_k) = (s_j, \chi)$, where χ is a string in Γ^*. If $\chi = \psi\gamma_k$ for some ψ in Γ^*, and thus $\delta(s_i, a, \gamma_k) = (s_j, \psi\gamma_k)$, then ψ is added to the store. Notice that the last added element is noted at the left.
(d) $\delta(s_i, a, \gamma_k) = (s_j, \lambda)$. Because λ is the null-string, this simply means that the top symbol γ_k is removed.

It can also occur that $\delta\ (s_i, a, \gamma_k) = \varphi$; the automaton is then said to BLOCK.

The function δ maps the cartesian product $S \times (I \cup \lambda) \times \Gamma$ in $S \times \Gamma^* \cup \varphi$.

A CONFIGURATION in a push-down automaton is a combination of state and store content. A transition rule in δ can bring the automaton from one configuration to another. If there is a rule $\delta(s_i, a, \gamma_k) = (s_j, \chi)$, then the introduction of the input element a can change the configuration from $(s_i, \gamma_k\omega)$ to $(s_j, \chi\omega)$. The notation for this is:

$$a\colon\ (s_i, \gamma_k\omega) \vdash (s_j, \chi\omega).$$

This change is called a TRANSITION in the automaton. Unless otherwise stated, we shall suppose that $\delta(s, \lambda, \gamma) = (s, \gamma)$ for every s in S and for every γ in Γ; in other words, the input of λ changes neither state nor store content. Thus:

$$\lambda\colon\ (s, \omega) \vdash (s, \omega) \text{ for every } s \in S \text{ and every } \omega \in \Gamma^*.$$

In specially mentioned cases where it is permitted that $\delta(s, \lambda, \gamma) \neq (s, \gamma)$ (i.e. where the automaton can make a real change of state without input), we must allow that $\delta(s, a, \gamma) = \varphi$ for every a in I, for otherwise the automaton could make various different transitions when the input a is introduced. The INITIAL CONFIGURATION of a push-down automaton is by definition (s_0, γ_0).

We write $x = a_1 a_2 \ldots a_n$: $(s, \omega) \overset{*}{\vdash} (s', \omega')$, if δ allows transitions a_i: $(s_i, \omega_i) \vdash (s_{i+1}, \omega_{i+1})$, where $i = 1, 2, \ldots, n$, such that $s_1 = s$, $\omega_1 = \omega$, $s_{n+1} = s'$, and $\omega_{n+1} = \omega'$. String x makes the automaton change from configuration (s, ω) to configuration (s', ω').

A string x is ACCEPTED by a *PDA* if at the end of the processing of x the push-down store is empty. Formally, string x is accepted by *PDA* if x: $(s_0, \gamma_0) \overset{*}{\vdash} (s, \lambda)$. Note that this definition is not based on the attainment of a final state, as was the case with finite automata. There exists a description of push-down automata which does refer to the attainment of a final state; it is completely equivalent to the description used here, and we shall not bring it into the discussion.

The LANGUAGE $T(PDA)$ accepted by a push-down automaton is the set of strings which are accepted by that automaton, $T(PDA) = \{x | x: (s_0, \gamma_0) \overset{*}{\vdash} (s, \lambda)\}$.

Figure 5.1 shows how a push-down automaton accepts a string.

EXAMPLE 5.1. In order to demonstrate the operation of the push-down automaton, we take a *PDA* which only uses its store, and never changes states. The automaton accepts strings of *a*'s, *b*'s, and *c*'s, with as many *a*'s as *b*'s, and one *c* at the end of the string: e.g. *c*, *abc*, *aabbc*, *baabc*, etc.

$PDA = (S, I, \Gamma, \delta, s_0, \gamma_0)$, with $S = \{s_0\}$, $I = \{a, b, c\}$, $\Gamma = \{\gamma_0, \gamma_a, \gamma_b\}$, and where δ consists of the following transition rules:

1. $\delta(s_0, a, \gamma_0) = (s_0, \gamma_a\gamma_0)$	5. $\delta(s_0, b, \gamma_b) = (s_0, \gamma_b\gamma_b)$
2. $\delta(s_0, a, \gamma_a) = (s_0, \gamma_a\gamma_a)$	6. $\delta(s_0, b, \gamma_a) = (s_0, \lambda)$
3. $\delta(s_0, a, \gamma_b) = (s_0, \lambda)$	7. $\delta(s_0, c, \gamma_0) = (s_0, \lambda)$
4. $\delta(s_0, b, \gamma_0) = (s_0, \gamma_b\gamma_0)$	For all other (s, c, γ), $\delta(s, c, \gamma) = \varphi$.

By convention $\delta\ (s, \lambda, \gamma) = (s, \gamma)$ for all s, γ.

We shall now show how the automaton accepts the string

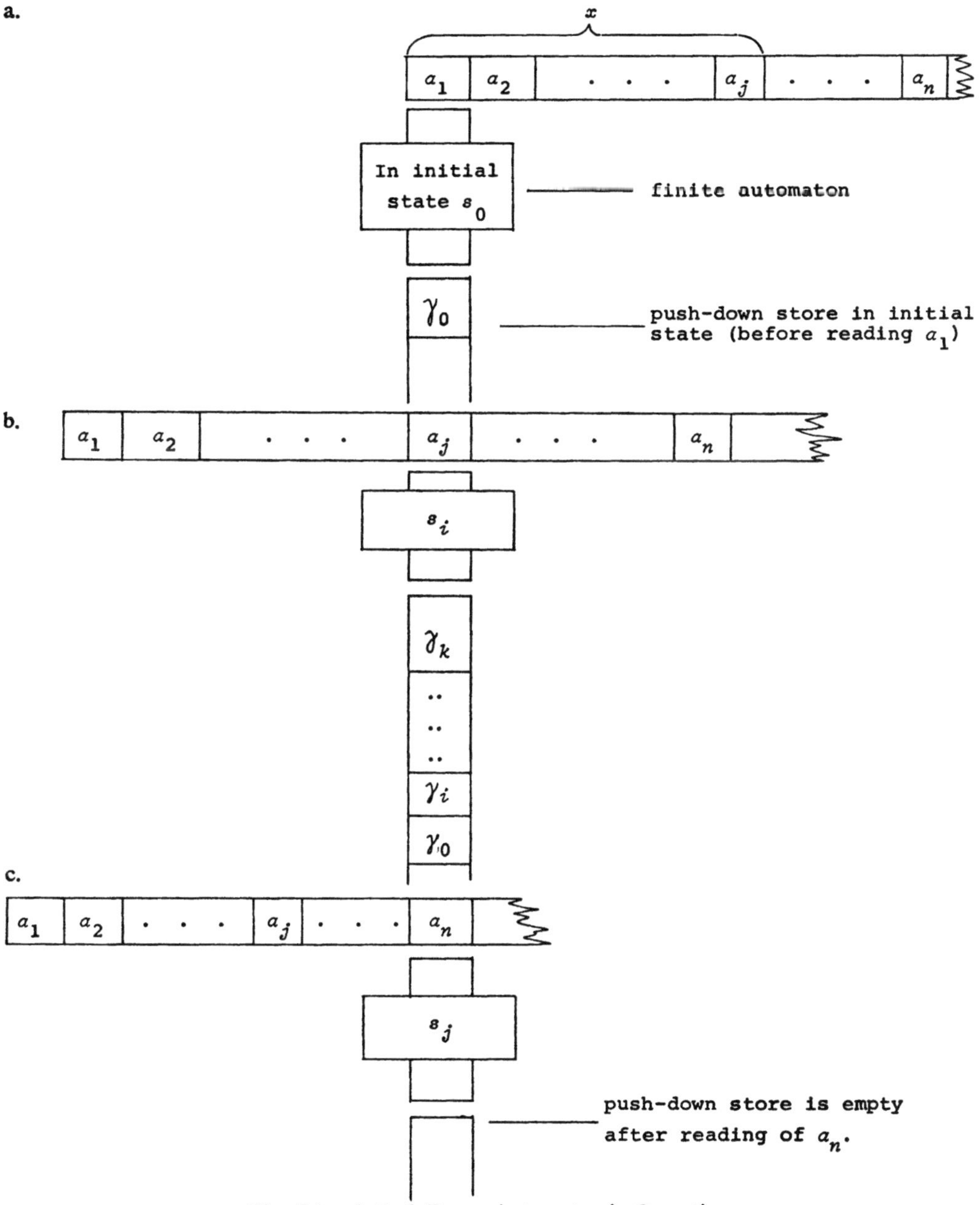

Fig. 5.1. A Push-Down Automaton in Operation
a. Situation at start
b. Automaton while processing string x
c. Automaton after accepting string x

aabbbbaac. The following list gives the successive transitions and the rules applied.

a: $(s_o, \gamma_o) \vdash (s_o, \gamma_a\gamma_o)$ (rule 1)
a: $(s_o, \gamma_a\gamma_o) \vdash (s_o, \gamma_a\gamma_a\gamma_o)$ (rule 2)
b: $(s_o, \gamma_a\gamma_a\gamma_o) \vdash (s_o, \gamma_a\gamma_o)$ (rule 6)
b: $(s_o, \gamma_a\gamma_o) \vdash (s_o, \gamma_o)$ (rule 6)
b: $(s_o, \gamma_o) \vdash (s_o, \gamma_b\gamma_o)$ (rule 4)
b: $(s_o, \gamma_b\gamma_o) \vdash (s_o, \gamma_b\gamma_b\gamma_o)$ (rule 5)
a: $(s_o, \gamma_b\gamma_b\gamma_o) \vdash (s_o, \gamma_b\gamma_o)$ (rule 3)
a: $(s_o, \gamma_b\gamma_o) \vdash (s_o, \gamma_o)$ (rule 3)
c: $(s_o, \gamma_o) \vdash (s_o, \lambda)$ (rule 7)

Thus $aabbbbaac$: $(s_o, \gamma_o) \vdash^* (s_o, \lambda)$.

EXAMPLE 5.2 Let $PDA = (S, I, \Gamma, \delta, s_o, \gamma_o)$ be a push-down automaton where $S = \{s_o, s_1\}$, $I = \{a, b, c\}$, $\Gamma = \{\gamma_o, \gamma_a, \gamma_b\}$, with the following transition rules:

1. $\delta(s_o, a, \gamma_o) = (s_o, \gamma_a\gamma_o)$
2. $\delta(s_o, a, \gamma_a) = (s_o, \gamma_a\gamma_a)$
3. $\delta(s_o, a, \gamma_b) = (s_o, \gamma_a\gamma_b)$
4. $\delta(s_o, b, \gamma_o) = (s_o, \gamma_b\gamma_o)$
5. $\delta(s_o, b, \gamma_b) = (s_o, \gamma_b\gamma_b)$
6. $\delta(s_o, b, \gamma_a) = (s_o, \gamma_b\gamma_a)$
7. $\delta(s_o, c, \gamma_o) = (s_o, \lambda)$
8. $\delta(s_o, c, \gamma_a) = (s_1, \gamma_a)$
9. $\delta(s_o, c, \gamma_b) = (s_1, \gamma_b)$
10. $\delta(s_1, a, \gamma_a) = (s_1, \lambda)$
11. $\delta(s_1, b, \gamma_b) = (s_1, \lambda)$
12. $\delta(s_1, \lambda, \gamma_o) = (s_1, \lambda)$

$\delta(s, \lambda, \gamma) = (s, \gamma)$ for every other s, γ and in all other cases $\delta(s, -, \gamma) = \varphi$.

This push-down automaton accepts all symmetric sentences, where c may occur only in the middle of the sentence. If w is a string of a's and b's, and w^R is the "mirror image" of w, then the language accepted by PDA is $\{wcw^R\}$. In essence, the PDA places a γ_a into the store for every incoming a, and a γ_b for every incoming b until a c is introduced. From that point the state changes from s_o to s_1, and the process is reversed: for every incoming a it removes the top symbol if it is γ_a, and for every incoming b it removes the top symbol if it is γ_b. This continues until γ_o is the top symbol, and by rule 12 the automaton removes γ_o without further input.

The sequence of transitions for string *aabbcbbaa* is as follows:

$(s_o, \gamma_o) \vdash (s_o, \gamma_a\gamma_o) \vdash (s_o, \gamma_b\gamma_a\gamma_o) \vdash (s_o, \gamma_b\gamma_b\gamma_a\gamma_o) \vdash (s_1, \gamma_b\gamma_b\gamma_a\gamma_o) \vdash$
$(s_1, \gamma_b\gamma_a\gamma_o) \vdash (s_1, \gamma_a\gamma_o) \vdash (s_1, \gamma_o) \vdash (s_1, \lambda)$.

It is obvious that push-down automata can do more than finite automata. The languages which are accepted by the automata in the last two examples are both context-free languages, and there is no finite automaton which can accept them. But push-down automata cannot accept all context-free languages; the languages which they accept are called DETERMINISTIC LANGUAGES. A class of grammars is known which generates precisely these deterministic languages, namely the class of $LR(k)$-GRAMMARS. These are equivalent to push-down automata. We shall not discuss $LR(k)$-grammars here. The interested reader may consult Knuth (1965).

However, there is equivalence between context-free languages and nondeterministic push-down automata.

5.2. NONDETERMINISTIC PUSH-DOWN AUTOMATA AND CONTEXT-FREE LANGUAGES

A nondeterministic push-down automaton *NPDA* differs from a *PDA* only in that each of its transition rules is of the following form:

$$\delta(s, a, \gamma) = \{(s_1, \gamma_1), (s_2, \gamma_2), \ldots, (s_n, \gamma_n)\}.$$

This means that in each configuration the automaton is not limited to a single possible transition, but can make a "choice" among the elements of a set of transitions.[1] The construction of a nondeterministic push-down automaton is completely analogous to that of a nondeterministic finite automaton, and the same is true of the definition of accepting. A *NPDA* ACCEPTS a string x, if, when x is

[1] At this point we drop the condition that if $\delta(s, \lambda, \gamma) \neq \varphi$, then $\delta(s, a, \gamma) = \varphi$ for every a in I. This condition was necessary in order to exclude the possibility of a nondeterministic transition when an input a is introduced into the automaton.

introduced as input, there is at least one possible sequence of transitions for which x: $(s_o, r_o) \vdash^* (s, \lambda)$.

EXAMPLE 5.3. Let us construct a simple *NPDA* which will accept the language $\{a^n b^n \mid n \geqslant 1\}$. Let $NPDA = (\{s_o\}, \{a, b\}, \{\gamma_o, \gamma_a, \gamma_b\}, \delta, s_o, \gamma_o)$, with the following transition rules in δ:

1. $\delta(s_o, \lambda, \gamma_o) = \{(s_o, \gamma_a\gamma_b), (s_o, \gamma_a\gamma_o\gamma_b)\}$
2. $\delta(s_o, a, \gamma_a) = \{(s_o, \lambda)\}$
3. $\delta(s_o, b, \gamma_b) = \{(s_o, \lambda)\}$

By convention, $\delta(s, \lambda, \gamma) = (s, \gamma)$ for every s and γ, and $\delta(s, -, \gamma) = \varphi$ for all other δ.

Only rule 1 is nondeterministic. To show how *NPDA* operates, we give the successive transitions in the accepting of the string *aaabbb*:

λ: $(s_o, \gamma_o) \vdash (s_o, \gamma_a\gamma_o\gamma_b)$	(rule 1)
a: $(s_o, \gamma_a\gamma_o\gamma_b) \vdash (s_o, \gamma_o\gamma_b)$	(rule 2)
λ: $(s_o, \gamma_o\gamma_b) \vdash (s_o, \gamma_a\gamma_o\gamma_b\gamma_b)$	(rule 1)
a: $(s_o, \gamma_a\gamma_o\gamma_b\gamma_b) \vdash (s_o, \gamma_o\gamma_b\gamma_b)$	(rule 2)
λ: $(s_o, \gamma_o\gamma_b\gamma_b) \vdash (s_o, \gamma_a\gamma_b\gamma_b\gamma_b)$	(rule 1)
a: $(s_o, \gamma_a\gamma_b\gamma_b\gamma_b) \vdash (s_o, \gamma_b\gamma_b\gamma_b)$	(rule 2)
b: $(s_o, \gamma_b\gamma_b\gamma_b) \vdash (s_o, \gamma_b\gamma_b)$	(rule 3)
b: $(s_o, \gamma_b\gamma_b) \vdash (s_o, \gamma_b)$	(rule 3)
b: $(s_o, \gamma_b) \vdash (s_o, \lambda)$	(rule 3)

Thus $aaabbb = \lambda a \lambda a \lambda abbb$: $(s_o, \gamma_o) \vdash^* (s_o, \lambda)$.

This example also shows how a push-down automaton can make spontaneous transitions (when the input is λ), and how the initial symbol γ_o can be removed from the store before the store is empty.

Theorems 5.1 and 5.2 together show the equivalence of nondeterministic push-down automata and context-free grammars.

THEOREM 5.1. For every context-free language L, there is a nondeterministic push-down automaton which accepts L and only L.

PROOF. In fact we shall prove a somewhat stronger theorem,

namely, that there is a nondeterministic push-down automaton with only one state which can accept the context-free language L.

Let L be a context-free language, and $G = (V_N, V_T, P, S)$, a grammar in Greibach normal-form which generates language L (according to Theorem 2.7., such a grammar exists). The productions in G are thus exclusively of the form $A \rightarrow a\alpha$, where α is a string of 0 or more variables. We construct a nondeterministic push-down automaton $NPDA = (S, I, \Gamma, \delta, s_o, \gamma_o)$ as follows: $S = \{s_o\}$, $I = V_T$ (with elements a_i), $\Gamma = V_N \cup V_T = V$ (with elements a_i in V_T and elements A_i, S in V_N), $\gamma_o = S$. The input vocabulary of $NPDA$ is the terminal vocabulary of G; the push-down symbols of $NPDA$ are the elements of V in G, and the push-down start symbol of $NPDA$ is the start symbol S of G. Let $NPDA$ have the following transition rules:

1. $\delta(s_o, \lambda, A)$ contains $(s_o, a\alpha)$ for every production $A \rightarrow a\alpha$ in P (where α can have length 0).
2. $\delta(s_o, a, a) = \{(s_o, \lambda)\}$ for every a in V_T.

The push-down automaton will in general be nondeterministic, for if A can be rewritten in more than one way in G (e.g. $A \rightarrow \alpha$ and $A \rightarrow \beta$), then $\delta(s_o, \lambda, A)$ likewise has more than one possible transition ((s_o, α) and (s_o, β) in the present example).

We must show that $T(NPDA) = L(G)$. We shall first show that if $x \in L(G)$, then $x \in L(NPDA)$; afterwards we shall show the inverse.

(1) If $x = a_1a_2 \dots a_n$ in $L(G)$, then $S \overset{*}{\Rightarrow} x$ with the following leftmost derivation: $S \Rightarrow a_1\alpha_1 \Rightarrow a_1a_2\alpha_2 \Rightarrow \dots \Rightarrow a_1a_2 \dots a_{n-1}A_{n-1} \Rightarrow a_1a_2 \dots a_n$. This derivation is performed by rewriting the leftmost variable of α_i at each step. If we wish explicitly to show this variable in the derivation, we can write $S \Rightarrow a_1A_1\beta_1 \Rightarrow a_1a_2A_2\beta_2 \Rightarrow \dots \Rightarrow a_1a_2 \dots a_{n-1}A_{n-1} \Rightarrow a_1a_2 \dots a_n$, where β_i represents the string of remaining variables. The following shows how $NPDA$ precisely simulates this leftmost derivation for $x = a_1a_2 \dots a_n$:

λ: $(s_o, S) \vdash (s_o, a_1A_1\beta_1)$ (rule 1)
a_1: $(s_o, a_1A_1\beta_1) \vdash (s_o, A_1\beta_1)$ (rule 2)

$$\begin{array}{rll} \lambda: & (s_o, A_1\beta_1) \vdash (s_o, a_2A_2\beta_2) & \text{(rule 1)} \\ a_2: & (s_o, a_2A_2\beta_2) \vdash (s_o, A_2\beta_2) & \text{(rule 2)} \\ & \vdots & \\ a_{n-1}: & (s_o, a_{n-1}A_{n-1}) \vdash (s_o, A_{n-1}) & \text{(rule 2)} \\ \lambda: & (s_o, A_{n-1}) \vdash (s_o, a_n) & \text{(rule 1)} \\ a_n: & (s_o, a_n) \vdash (s_o, \lambda) & \text{(rule 2)} \end{array}$$

Thus $x \in T(NPDA)$.

(2) If $x = b_1b_2 \ldots b_m$ is accepted by $NPDA$, then $b_i \in I$. The transitions in $NPDA$ in accepting x take place when the input b is introduced, or "spontaneously" when the input is λ. We can therefore write $x = a_1a_2 \ldots a_n$, where $a_i = \lambda$, or $a_i = b_j$, while maintaining the order and in such a way that exactly one transition of $NPDA$ goes together with each a_i in the acceptance of x. Thus we have the following steps for accepting x:

$$\begin{array}{rl} a_1: & (s_o, S) \vdash (s_o, \omega_1) \\ a_2: & (s_o, \omega_1) \vdash (s_o, \omega_2) \\ & \vdots \\ a_n: & (s_o, \omega_{n-1}) \vdash (s_o, \lambda) \end{array}$$

With regard to rule 2, it follows directly that $\omega_{n-1} = a_n$, and tritely $\omega_{n-1} \overset{*}{\Rightarrow} a_n$ in grammar G. We shall now take as an inductive hypothesis that $\omega_i \overset{*}{\Rightarrow} a_{i+1} \ldots a_n$ in G, and show that $\omega_{i-1} \Rightarrow a_i \ldots a_n$. It then follows by induction (going back to $n-1$, for which the theorem is valid) that $\omega_o = S \overset{*}{\Rightarrow} a_1 \ldots a_n$.

We thus suppose that $\omega_i \overset{*}{\Rightarrow} a_{i+1} \ldots a_n$. We know that a_i: $(s_o, \omega_{i-1}) \vdash (s_o, \omega_i)$. There are two possibilities: $a_i \in V_T$ or $a_i = \lambda$. Let us first suppose that $a_i \in V_T$. In that case the transition a_i: $(s_o, \omega_{i-1}) \vdash (s_o, \omega_i)$ can only have taken place by means of rule 2, and consequently $\omega_{i-1} = a_i\omega_i$. But because $\omega_i \overset{*}{\Rightarrow} a_{i+1} \ldots a_n$ (induction hypothesis), it is true that $\omega_{i-1} = a_i\omega_i \overset{*}{\Rightarrow} a_ia_{i+1} \ldots a_n$, that which we had to prove.

Now let us suppose that $a_i = \lambda$. In this case the transition $a_i = \lambda$: $(s_o, \omega_{i-1}) \vdash (s_o, \omega_i)$ can only have taken place by means of rule 1, and consequently $\omega_{i-1} = A\omega'_{i-1}$ and $\omega_i = a\alpha\omega'_{i-1}$. Because A $\rightarrow a\alpha$ is by definition a production in G, it is true that $A\omega'_{i-1} \Rightarrow a\alpha\omega'_{i-1}$, or otherwise formulated $\omega_{i-1} \Rightarrow \omega_i$. According to the induction hypothesis, however, $\omega_i = a_{i+1} \dots a_n$, and consequently we have the following derivation: $\omega_{i-1} \Rightarrow a_{i+1} \dots a_n = \lambda a_{i+1} \dots a_n = a_i a_{i+1} \dots a_n$, which is what we had to prove. We conclude, then, that $\omega_o = S \overset{*}{\Rightarrow} x$.

To illustrate Theorem 5.1., we offer the following example.

EXAMPLE 5.4. Take context-free language $L = \{a^n cb^n\}$, $n \geqslant 0$. A simple grammar for L is $G = (\{S, B\}, \{a, b, c\}, \{S \rightarrow aSB, B \rightarrow b, S \rightarrow c\}, S)$, which is in Greibach normal-form. According to the procedure given in the proof of Theorem 5.1., we construct the following push-down automaton which accepts language L: $NPDA = (S, I, \Gamma, \delta, s_0, \gamma_0)$, with $S = \{s_0\}$, $I = V_T = \{a, b, c\}$, $\Gamma = V = \{a, b, c, S, B\}$, $\gamma_0 = S$, and with the following transition rules in δ:

1. $\delta(s_0, \lambda, S) = \{(s_0, aSB), (s_0, c)\}$
2. $\delta(s_0, \lambda, B) = \{(s_0, b)\}$
3. $\delta(s_0, a, a) = \{(s_0, \lambda)\}$
4. $\delta(s_0, b, b) = \{(s_0, \lambda)\}$
5. $\delta(s_0, c, c) = \{(s_0, \lambda)\}$

The following list shows the various steps by which $NPDA$ accepts the sentence $aacbb$:

λ: $(s_0, S) \vdash (s_0, aSB)$	(rule 1)
a: $(s_0, aSB) \vdash (s_0, SB)$	(rule 3)
λ: $(s_0, SB) \vdash (s_0, aSBB)$	(rule 1)
a: $(s_0, aSBB) \vdash (s_0, SBB)$	(rule 3)
λ: $(s_0, SBB) \vdash (s_0, cBB)$	(rule 1)
c: $(s_0, cBB) \vdash (s_0, BB)$	(rule 5)
λ: $(s_0, BB) \vdash (s_0, bB)$	(rule 2)
b: $(s_0, bB) \vdash (s_0, B)$	(rule 4)
λ: $(s_0, B) \vdash (s_0, b)$	(rule 2)
b: $(s_0, b) \vdash (s_0, \lambda)$	(rule 4)

To complete the proof of equivalence between nondeterministic push-down automata and context-free grammars, we must prove the following theorem.

THEOREM 5.2. For every language T which is accepted by a non-deterministic push-down automaton, there is a context-free grammar G which generates precisely T.

PROOF. Let T be the language accepted by $NPDA = (S, I, \Gamma, \delta, s_o, \gamma_o)$. We must construct a context-free grammar $G = (V_N, V_T, P, S)$ as follows:

(i) V_N consists of compound elements $[s_i, \gamma, s_j]$, where s_i and s_j are elements of S, and γ is an element of Γ. V_N also contains S, which is not compound.

(ii) $V_T = I$.

(iii) P contains the following productions:

1. $S \rightarrow [s_o, \gamma_o, s]$ for every s in S.
2. $\{[s, \gamma, s_{n+1}] \rightarrow a[s_1, \gamma_1, s_2]\,[s_2, \gamma_2, s_3] \ldots [s_n, \gamma_n, s_{n+1}]$ for any numbering of states in $S\}$ for every transition rule in δ of the form: $\delta(s, a, \gamma)$ contains $(s_1, \gamma_1\gamma_2 \ldots \gamma_n)$.

The second rule gives productions in G for every transition rule in $NPDA$. These productions are in Greibach normal-form: to the right of the arrow there is a terminal element followed by 0 or more variables. The case of 0 variables occurs when $\gamma_1\gamma_2 \ldots \gamma_n = \lambda$, thus in transition rules in which $\delta(s, a, \gamma)$ includes (s_1, λ); this gives the following productions in G: $[s, \gamma, s_i] \rightarrow a$ for all s_i in S.

Although the first production is not Greibach normal-form, every leftmost derivation of G is as follows: $S \Rightarrow \alpha_o \Rightarrow a_1\alpha_1 \Rightarrow a_1a_2\alpha_2 \Rightarrow \ldots \Rightarrow a_1a_2 \ldots a_n$, where every α is a string of variables. Each of these variables is composed of three elements. If we examine the components γ in these variables, we find that they stand for every α_i precisely in the order they take on in the push-down store when $a_1a_2 \ldots a_i$ is introduced into the automaton. Thus the grammar simulates the push-down automaton. Before continuing the proof of the theorem, we present an example in which this simulation is clearly to be seen.

EXAMPLE 5.5. Let $NPDA = (S, I, \Gamma, \delta, s_o, \gamma_o)$ be a nondeterministic push-down automaton with $S = \{s_o, s_1\}$, $I = \{a, b\}$,

$\Gamma = \{\gamma_o, \gamma_1\}$, and the transition rules given in Table 5.1. We must construct a grammar $G = (V_N, V_T, P, S)$ according to the above procedure: V_N consists of S and all triples $[s_i, a \vee b, s_j]$. For convenience we use a separate upper case letter to denote each of these compound variables:

$$A = [s_o, \gamma_o, s_o],\ B = [s_o, \gamma_o, s_1],\ C = [s_o, \gamma_1, s_o],\ D = [s_o, \gamma_1, s_1],$$
$$E = [s_1, \gamma_o, s_o],\ F = [s_1, \gamma_o, s_1],\ G = [s_1, \gamma_1, s_o],\ H = [s_1, \gamma_1, s_1].$$

Further $V_T = \{a, b\}$; the productions are given in Table 5.1. in both complete and abbreviated notation, grouped according to the corresponding transition rules. The abbreviated notation clearly shows that only the numbered productions lead to terminal strings.

TABLE 5.1. Transition Rules of *NPDA* and Corresponding Productions of Equivalent Grammar *G* (Example 5.5.).

Transition Rules *NPDA*	Productions *G*	Abbreviated Notation
	1. $S \rightarrow [s_o, \gamma_o, s_o]$	$S \rightarrow A$
	2. $S \rightarrow [s_o, \gamma_o, s_1]$	$S \rightarrow B$
(a) $\delta(s_o, a, \gamma_1) = \{(s_1,\gamma_1)\}$	$[s_o, \gamma_1, s_o] \rightarrow a[s_1, \gamma_1, s_o]$	$C \rightarrow aG$
	3. $[s_o, \gamma_1, s_1] \rightarrow a[s_1, \gamma_1, s_1]$	$D \rightarrow aH$
(b) $\delta(s_o, b, \gamma_o) = \{(s_o, \gamma_1\gamma_o)\}$	$[s_o,\gamma_o,s_o] \rightarrow b[s_o,\gamma_1,s_o]\ [s_o,\gamma_o,s_o]$	$A \rightarrow bCA$
	4. $[s_o,\gamma_o,s_o] \rightarrow b[s_o,\gamma_1,s_1]\ [s_1,\gamma_o,s_o]$	$A \rightarrow bDE$
	$[s_o,\gamma_o,s_1] \rightarrow b[s_o,\gamma_1,s_o]\ [s_o,\gamma_o,s_1]$	$B \rightarrow bCB$
	5. $[s_o,\gamma_o,s_1] \rightarrow b[s_o,\gamma_1,s_1]\ [s_1,\gamma_o,s_1]$	$B \rightarrow bDF$
(c) $\delta(s_o, b, \gamma_1) = \{(s_o, \gamma_1\gamma_1)\}$	$[s_o,\gamma_1,s_o] \rightarrow b[s_o,\gamma_1,s_o]\ [s_o,\gamma_1,s_o]$	$C \rightarrow bCC$
	$[s_o,\gamma_1,s_o] \rightarrow b[s_o,\gamma_1,s_1]\ [s_1,\gamma_1,s_o]$	$C \rightarrow bDG$
	$[s_o,\gamma_1,s_1] \rightarrow b[s_o,\gamma_1,s_o]\ [s_o,\gamma_1,s_1]$	$D \rightarrow bCD$
	6. $[s_o,\gamma_1,s_1] \rightarrow b[s_o,\gamma_1,s_1]\ [s_1,\gamma_1,s_1]$	$D \rightarrow bDH$
(d) $\delta(s_o, \lambda, \gamma_o) = \{(s_o, \lambda)\}$	7. $[s_o, \gamma_o, s_o] \rightarrow \lambda$	$A \rightarrow \lambda$
(e) $\delta(s_1, a, \gamma_o) = \{(s_o, \gamma_o)\}$	8. $[s_1, \gamma_o, s_o] \rightarrow a[s_o, \gamma_o, s_o]$	$E \rightarrow aA$
	9. $[s_1, \gamma_o, s_1] \rightarrow a[s_o, \gamma_o, s_1]$	$F \rightarrow aB$
(f) $\delta(s_1, b, \gamma_1) = \{(s_1, \lambda)\}$	10. $[s_1, \gamma_1, s_1] \rightarrow b$	$H \rightarrow b$
	$[s_1, \gamma_1, s_o] \rightarrow b$	$G \rightarrow b$

In order to show how G simulates *NPDA*, we give first the acceptance of the sentence *bbabba* by *NPDA*, and then the generation of the same sentence by G. Acceptance by *NPDA*:

b: $(s_0, \gamma_0) \vdash (s_0, \gamma_1\gamma_0)$	(rule b)
b: $(s_0, \gamma_1\gamma_0) \vdash (s_0, \gamma_1\gamma_1\gamma_0)$	(rule c)
a: $(s_0, \gamma_1\gamma_1\gamma_0) \vdash (s_1, \gamma_1\gamma_1\gamma_0)$	(rule a)
b: $(s_1, \gamma_1\gamma_1\gamma_0) \vdash (s_1, \gamma_1\gamma_0)$	(rule f)
b: $(s_1, \gamma_1\gamma_0) \vdash (s_1, \gamma_0)$	(rule f)
a: $(s_1, \gamma_0) \vdash (s_0, \gamma_0)$	(rule e)
λ: $(s_0, \gamma_0) \vdash (s_0, \lambda)$	(rule d)

Derivation by G:

$S \Rightarrow A$	(production 1)
$A \Rightarrow bDE$	(production 4)
$bDE \Rightarrow bbDHE$	(production 6)
$bbDHE \Rightarrow bbaHHE$	(production 3)
$bbaHHE \Rightarrow bbabHE$	(production 10)
$bbabHE \Rightarrow bbabbE$	(production 10)
$bbabbE \Rightarrow bbabbaA$	(production 8)
$bbabbaA \Rightarrow bbabba$	(production 7)

It should be noticed that the last step in this derivation is an abbreviation although this is theoretically not permitted with a context-free grammar. The abbreviation is a result of production 7 in Table 5.1, but this production is actually only a formalization of the convention introduced in paragraph 2.1., that λ can be added to a context-free language.

We can now continue with the proof of Theorem 5.2. We must show that $T(NPDA) = L(G)$. The proof follows two steps: first we must show that if $x \in T$, then x is also generated by G; then we must show the inverse of this statement.

(1) If $x = a_1a_2 \ldots a_m$ is in $T(NPDA)$, then $S \overset{*}{\Rightarrow} x$. To prove this we must show by induction that for every n the following is true: if x: $(s_i, \gamma) \overset{*}{\vdash} (s, \lambda)$ in n transitions, then $[s_i, \gamma, s_j] \overset{*}{\Rightarrow} x$ by the productions of G. We first prove the theorem for $n = 1$, then show that it is also valid for $n - 1$ or fewer steps, and consequently

that it holds for n steps; thence follows general validity. From that point it is not difficult to show that if x is accepted by *NPDA*, then it is also generated by G.

If $n = 1$, then either $x = a$ (where $a \in I$), or $x = \lambda$. In both cases $x: (s_i, \gamma) \vdash (s_j, \lambda)$, and therefore (s_i, x, γ) must include (s_j, λ), so that G (according to production 2) includes the production $[s_i, \gamma, s_j] \rightarrow x$. It follows directly that $[s_i, \gamma, s_j] \Rightarrow x$ is a derivation of G.

Let us now suppose that the theorem holds for fewer than n transition steps. Let us examine $x = a_1a_2 \ldots a_m$ $(m \geqslant 0)$, for which $x: (s_i, \gamma) \overset{*}{\vdash} (s_j, \lambda)$ in precisely n transitions. The first step in this process is as follows: $a: (s_i, \gamma) \vdash (s_1, \gamma_1\gamma_2 \ldots \gamma_k)$. The element a here is either λ, or the first element a_1 of x. After the first step, the push-down store thus contains $\gamma_1\gamma_2 \ldots \gamma_k$, and $n - 1$ transitions remain to be made before this string is completely removed from the store. We know that this does finally occur, and that the respective γ_i's are successively removed. This, however, need not proceed directly, and might, on the contrary, follow various detours (γ_i might, for example, be replaced by a whole string of new push-down symbols, which will be removed when latter elements of x are introduced into the input). Nevertheless it must remain possible to articulate the string $x = a_1a_2 \ldots a_m$ in such a way that it can be written as $aw_1w_2 \ldots w_k$ where $a = \lambda$ or $a = a_1$ (dependent on the nature of the first step), and where every w_i leads to the removal of γ_i, when the operation on the step began in the proper state s_i. But if γ_i can be removed from the store with w_i as input, then it also holds that if γ_i should be the only element in the push-down store while the automaton is in state s_i, $w_i: (s_i, \gamma_i) \overset{*}{\vdash} (s_{i+1}, \lambda)$, where s_{i+1} is precisely the state beginning with which w_{i+1} would empty the store if only γ_{i+1} were in it. For every w this process of emptying takes fewer than n steps, and there are productions in G such that $[s_i, \gamma_i, s_{i+1}] \overset{*}{\Rightarrow} w_i$ (induction hypothesis). It holds also that the string of variables $[s_1, \gamma_1, s_2]$ $[s_2, \gamma_2, s_3] \ldots [s_k, \gamma_k, s_{k+1}]$ can be rewritten by means of the productions in G as the terminal string $w_1w_2 \ldots w_k$. From $a: (s_i, \gamma) \vdash$ $(s_1, \gamma_1\gamma_2 \ldots \gamma_k)$, however, we know that $(s_1, \gamma_1\gamma_2 \ldots \gamma_k)$ is an element of $\delta(s_i, a, \gamma)$, and therefore G (according to production 2) includes the production $[s_i, \gamma, s_{k+1}] \rightarrow a[s_1, \gamma_1, s_2]\,[s_2, \gamma_2, s_3] \ldots [s_k, \gamma_k, s_{k+1}]$. It therefore holds that $[s_i, \gamma, s_{k+1}] \overset{*}{\Rightarrow} aw_1w_2 \ldots w_k = x$, from which we see that the theorem also holds for n transitions. By induction, the theorem is valid in general.

It is true of every x which is accepted by $NPDA$ that x: $(s_o, \gamma_o) \vdash^* (s, \lambda)$, and consequently, by the theorem as proven, $[s_o, \gamma_o, s] \overset{*}{\Rightarrow} x$ in G. According to production 1, $S \rightarrow [s_o, \gamma_o, s]$ for every s in S; therefore $S \overset{*}{\Rightarrow} x$.

(2) If $S \overset{*}{\Rightarrow} x$, then $x \in T(NPDA)$. We shall first prove that for every $n > 0$, if $[s_i, \gamma, s_j] \overset{*}{\Rightarrow} x$ in G in n transitions, then x: $(s_i, \gamma) \vdash^* (s_j, \lambda)$ in $NPDA$. Let $n = 1$. Then $[s_i, \gamma, s_j] \rightarrow x$ is a production of G, and consequently, given the construction of G, either $x \in V_T$ or $x = \lambda$. Likewise $\delta(s_i, x, \gamma)$ includes (s_j, λ), from which follows that the theorem holds for $n = 1$.

Let the theorem hold for derivations in G with fewer than n steps (induction hypothesis). Let $[s, \gamma, t] \overset{*}{\Rightarrow} x = a_1a_2 \ldots a_m$ be a derivation which demands exactly n steps. This is possible, given the form of production 2, if a leftmost derivation is as follows: $[s, \gamma, t] \Rightarrow a[t_1]\,[t_2] \ldots [t_k] \overset{*}{\Rightarrow} aw_1[t_2]\,[t_3] \ldots [t_k] \overset{*}{\Rightarrow} \ldots \overset{*}{\Rightarrow} aw_1w_2 \ldots w_k = a_1a_2 \ldots a_m = x$. Here $[t_i]$ represents the triad $[s_i, \gamma_i, s_{i+1}]$, and w_i is a string of one or more successive elements a from x. Every w_i can be derived from $[t_i]$ by the productions of G, and in general $[t_i] \overset{*}{\Rightarrow} w_i$ in fewer than n steps. On the basis of the induction hypothesis, however, w_i: $(s_i, \gamma_i) \vdash^* (s_{i+1}, \lambda)$ for every $i = 1, \ldots, k$. But then it is also the case that $w_1w_2 \ldots w_k$: $(s_1, \gamma_1\gamma_2 \ldots \gamma_k) \vdash^* (s_2, \gamma_2 \ldots \gamma_k) \vdash^* \ldots \vdash^* (s_{k+1}, \lambda)$, and consequently also x: $(s, \gamma) \vdash^* (t = s_{k+1}, \lambda)$. By induction, the theorem holds for every $n > 0$.

The derivation $S \overset{*}{\Rightarrow} x$ can be written $S \Rightarrow [s_o, \gamma_o, s] \overset{*}{\Rightarrow} x$. If x is generated by G, then $[s_o, \gamma_o, s] \overset{*}{\Rightarrow} x$, so that, on the basis of the theorem x: $(s_o, \gamma_o) \vdash^* (s, \lambda)$, which by definition means that $x \in T(NPDA)$.

It follows from Theorems 5.1. and 5.2. that the class of languages which are accepted by nondeterministic push-down automata is precisely the same as the class of languages generated by context-free grammars.

6

LINEAR BOUNDED AUTOMATA

An automaton has been discovered which accepts precisely the languages of the context-sensitive class. Like the push-down automaton, it is unlimited, but in an interesting way. In effect, it disposes of as much storage capacity as the input string is long: the store is small for a short string, large for a long string. It is as if one had to calculate the sum of two numbers and were given exactly the same amount of space on a blackboard for counting as the two original numbers occupy. One would be allowed to write and to erase as often as desired, but could use no more space than that allowed.

The automaton in question is called LINEAR BOUNDED AUTOMATON, *LBA*. In this chapter we shall show that linear bounded automata are equivalent to context-sensitive grammars. But the proof of this equivalence is considerably more complicated than those in the preceding chapters, and we will not be able to discuss it fully within the scope of this book. Therefore we shall limit ourselves here to a global proof of the theorem that for every context-sensitive grammar there is an equivalent linear bounded automaton. We have chosen this particular theorem for proof because it refers to the Kuroda normal-form which will be used later in dealing with linguistic applications (in Volume II), and because it provides a good illustration of the way linear bounded automata work.

6.1. DEFINITIONS AND CONCEPTS

In several ways linear bounded automata resemble finite automata. In chapter 4 we observed that finite automata begin operating in an initial state and first read the leftmost symbol on the input tape. They then proceed to read the input symbols from left to right, until a final state is reached. Like finite automata, linear bounded automata also have a limited number of states, and they too begin their operation in an initial state by reading the leftmost symbol on the input tape. But linear bounded automata are capable of more than finite automata in two respects. In the first place, they can both read and write: they can write over a symbol which they have read, and replace it with another symbol. In the second place, they can move the input tape not only from left to right, but also from right to left; moreover, at a transition (a change of state and or the replacement of a symbol in the input tape), they can remain at the same position on the tape. In writing they can use "auxiliary symbols" which are not part of the input vocabulary. Because linear bounded automata may write only within the bondaries of the original input string, two boundary symbols (#) are placed on the tape, to the left of the first element and to the right of the last. Linear bounded automata always start in an initial state at the left-hand boundary symbol; they are said to accept the input when they pass over the right-hand boundary symbol in a final state. This latter is possible, of course, only after they have dealt with each element between the boundary symbols. The formal definitions are as follows.

A linear bounded automaton is a system $LBA = (S, I, \Gamma, \delta, s_0, \#, F)$ in which:

(1) S is a finite, nonempty set of STATES, with $s_0 \in S$ as INITIAL STATE, and $F \in S$ as the set of FINAL STATES. (States are, as usual, denoted by the letter s with a subscript, or by r, s, t, ...)

(2) I is a finite INPUT-VOCABULARY (notation as usual).

(3) Γ is a finite set of TAPE SYMBOLS, the vocabulary of symbols which can appear on the tape. I belongs to this set, as do all auxiliary symbols which can be used in writing. (Notation: tape

symbols are in general denoted by γ with a subscript; strings of auxiliary symbols are denoted by lower case letters from the end of the Greek alphabet, χ, ψ, ω. If it is known that a tape symbol belongs to the input vocabulary, the notation for I can be used.) There is also a special tape symbol #, the BOUNDARY SYMBOL.

(4) δ is a finite set of TRANSITION RULES. A transition rule indicates for a pair of state and tape symbols what the following state and tape symbol will be; it also indicates if the band remains at the same place, goes one place to the right, or one place to the left. This is written as follows: we say that (s_m, γ_n, k) is *in* $\delta(s_i, \gamma_j)$ if the automaton, in state s_i and reading γ_j, *can change* to state s_m and write γ_n in the place of γ_j. The letter k shows in which direction the automaton moves on the tape: $k = -1$ indicates that it goes to the left; $k = 1$ indicates that it goes to the right; $k = 0$ indicates that it remains in the same place and reads the symbol it has written in the place of γ_n. By convention, $\delta(s, \gamma)$ always contains $(s, \gamma, 0)$. We say "can change" because linear bounded automata are nondeterministic; a linear bounded automaton has in principal several possible transitions for each configuration. δ maps the cartesian product $S \times \Gamma$ in subsets of $S \times \Gamma \times \{-1, 0, 1\} \cup \varphi$. In every operation the boundary symbols must remain in place; thus, whenever the automaton reads # it writes # over it. In formal terms, if (s', γ, k) is in $\delta(s, \#)$, then $\gamma = \#$ for every s', and vice versa if $(s', \#, k)$ is in $\delta(s, \gamma)$, then $\gamma = \#$.

The concept of "configuration" calls for some further clarification. This can best be done with a visual representation of the operation of a linear bounded automaton, as in Figure 6.1. In that figure we see the initial and final situations in the process of accepting the string $x = a_1a_2 \ldots a_n$, as well as two possible situations during the operation.

A useful way of showing the entire configuration of automaton and tape is to write the state of the automaton to the left of the symbol which is being read. The configuration in Figure 6.1.a. can thus be denoted by $s_o\#a_1 \ldots a_n\#$ because the automaton is in state s_o and is reading the left-hand boundary symbol. For the configuration in Figure 6.1.b. we write $\#\gamma_1\gamma_2 \ldots \gamma_k s_j a_{k+1} \ldots a_n\#$,

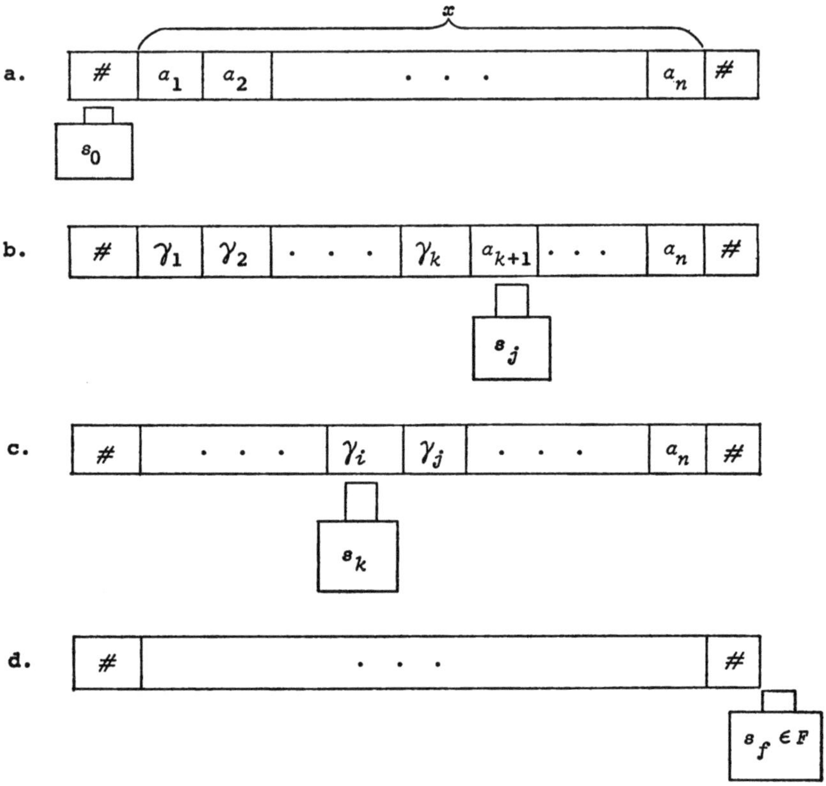

Fig. 6.1. A Linear Bounded Automaton in Operation

a. Situation at start.
b. } Possible situations during operation.
c. }
d. Situation after accepting x.

in which we see that the tape symbol a_{k+1} is being read in state s_j. The configuration in Figure 6.1.c. is written $\# \ldots s_k\gamma_i\gamma_j \ldots a_n\#$; that represented in Figure 6.1.d. is written $\# \ldots \#s_f$. If the automaton passes from configuration C to configuration C' in one step we write $C \vdash C'$, and when the change takes place by an undetermined number of transitions, the notation is $C \overset{*}{\vdash} C'$.

A linear bounded automaton *LBA* ACCEPTS a string x when

$s_o\#x\# \overset{*}{\vdash} \#\omega\#s_f$, where $x \in \mathrm{I}^*$, $\omega \in \Gamma^*$, and $s_f \in \mathrm{F}$. The LANGUAGE $T(LBA)$ accepted by LBA is the set of strings which are accepted by LBA: $T(LBA) = \{x | s_o\#x\# \overset{*}{\vdash} \#\omega\#s_f,\ x \in \mathrm{I}^*,\ \omega \in \Gamma^*,\ s_f \in \mathrm{F}\}$.

EXAMPLE 6.1. Let $LBA = (S, I, \Gamma, \delta, s_o, \#, F)$ be a linear bounded automaton in which $S = \{s_o, s_1, s_2, s_3, s_4, s_f\}$, $I = \{a, b\}$, $\Gamma = \{a, b, \gamma_a, \gamma_b, \#\}$, $F = \{s_f\}$, and with the following transition rules in δ:

1. $\delta(s_o, \#) = \{(s_1, \#, 1)\}$	7. $\delta(s_2, \gamma_b) = \{(s_3, \gamma_b, -1)\}$
2. $\delta(s_1, a) = \{(s_2, \gamma_a, 1)\}$	8. $\delta(s_2, \#) = \{(s_3, \#, -1)\}$
3. $\delta(s_1, \#) = \{(s_f, \#, 1)\}$	9. $\delta(s_3, b) = \{(s_4, \gamma_b, -1)\}$
4. $\delta(s_1, \gamma_b) = \{(s_1, \gamma_b, 1)\}$	10. $\delta(s_4, a) = \{(s_4, a, -1)\}$
5. $\delta(s_2, a) = \{(s_2, a, 1)\}$	11. $\delta(s_4, b) = \{(s_4, b, -1)\}$
6. $\delta(s_2, b) = \{(s_2, b, 1)\}$	12. $\delta(s_4, \gamma_a) = \{(s_1, \gamma_a, 1)\}$

$\delta(s, \gamma) = \varphi$ for all other cases for which no convention holds.

It is immediately obvious that this automaton is deterministic: there is never more than one possible transition. We shall first show how the automaton accepts the string *ab*. The input tape carries the string $\#ab\#$, and the first configuration is $s_o\#ab\#$, i.e. LBA is reading the left-hand boundary symbol in the initial state s_o. The successive steps are as follows:

$s_o\#ab\# \vdash \#s_1ab\#$	(rule 1)
$\#s_1ab\# \vdash \#\gamma_a s_2 b\#$	(rule 2)
$\#\gamma_a s_2 b\# \vdash \#\gamma_a b s_2\#$	(rule 6)
$\#\gamma_a b s_2\# \vdash \#\gamma_a s_3 b\#$	(rule 8)
$\#\gamma_a s_3 b\# \vdash \#s_4\gamma_a\gamma_b\#$	(rule 9)
$\#s_4\gamma_a\gamma_b\# \vdash \#\gamma_a s_1\gamma_b\#$	(rule 12)
$\#\gamma_a s_1\gamma_b\# \vdash \#\gamma_a\gamma_b s_1\#$	(rule 4)
$\#\gamma_a\gamma_b s_1\# \vdash \gamma\#_a\gamma_b\#s_f$	(rule 3)

The following shows in short how the automaton accepts the string *aabb*: $s_o\#aabb\# \vdash \#s_1aabb\# \vdash \#\gamma_a s_2 abb\# \overset{*}{\vdash} \#\gamma_a abb s_2\# \vdash \#\gamma_a ab s_3 b\# \vdash \#\gamma_a a s_4 b\gamma_b\# \overset{*}{\vdash} \#s_4\gamma_a ab\gamma_b\# \vdash \#\gamma_a s_1 ab\gamma_b\# \vdash \#\gamma_a\gamma_a s_2 b\gamma_b\# \vdash \#\gamma_a\gamma_a b s_2\gamma_b\# \vdash \#\gamma_a\gamma_a s_3 b\gamma_b\# \vdash \#\gamma_a s_4\gamma_a\gamma_b\gamma_b\# \vdash \#\gamma_a\gamma_a s_1\gamma_b\gamma_b\# \overset{*}{\vdash} \#\gamma_a\gamma_a\gamma_b\gamma_b\#s_f$.

Thus this automaton shifts back and forth between the boundary symbols until every a has been converted into γ_a, and every b into γ_b. It can reach the final state s_f only if there are as many γ_a's as γ_b's, and when the γ_a's are in the left-hand half of the tape, and the γ_b's in the right hand half. This automaton accepts the language $\{a^n b^n \mid n \geqslant 0\}$.

6.2. LINEAR BOUNDED AUTOMATA AND CONTEXT-SENSITIVE GRAMMARS

The equivalence of linear bounded automata and context-sensitive grammars is established in Theorems 6.1. and 6.2.

THEOREM 6.1. For every context-sensitive language L, there is a linear bounded automaton which accepts L and only L.

PROOF (summarized). Let L be a context-sensitive language. According to Theorem 2.11., there is a grammar G in Kuroda normal-form which generates L. We must construct a linear bounded automaton such that $T(LBA) = L(G)$. Let $G = (V_N, V_T, P, S)$. The automaton $LBA = (S, I, \Gamma, \delta, s_o, \#, F)$ must have the following construction:

(i) $S = \{s_o, s_1, t_o, t_1, \{t_A\}, r_o, r_1\}$, with s_o as both initial and final state: $F = \{s_o\}$.

(ii) $I = V_T$

(iii) $\Gamma = V_N \cup V_T \cup \#$

(iv) δ contains the following transition rules:

1. $\delta(s_o, \#) = \{(s_1, \#, 1)\}$	
2. $\delta(s_1, a) = \{(s_1, a, 1)\}$	for every a in V_T
3. $\delta(s_1, \#) = \{(t_o, \#, -1)\}$	
4. $\delta(t_o, A)$ contains $(t_o, A, 1)$	for every A in V_N
5. $\delta(t_o, A)$ contains $(t_o, A, -1)$	for every A in V_N
6. $\delta(t_o, a)$ contains $(t_o, a, 1)$	for every a in V_T
7. $\delta(t_o, a)$ contains $(t_o, a, -1)$	for every a in V_T
8. $\delta(t_o, B)$ contains $(t_o, A, 0)$	for all productions $A \rightarrow B$ in P

9. $\delta(t_o, a)$ contains $(t_o, A, 0)$		for all productions $A \to a$ in P
10. $\delta(t_o, C)$ contains $(t_A, A, 1)$	}	for all productions $AB \to CD$ in P
11. $\delta(t_A, D)$ contains $(t_o, B, 0)$		
12. $\delta(t_o, S)$ contains $(r_o, S, -1)$		
13. $\delta(r_o, \#) = \{(r_1, \#, 1)\}$		
14. $\delta(r_1, S) = \{(t_1, \#, 1)\}$	}	for all productions $S \to SA$ in P
15. $\delta(t_1, A) = \{(t_o, S, 0)\}$		
16. $\delta(t_1, \#) = \{(s_o, \#, 1)\}$		

In all other cases where no convention holds, $\delta(s, \gamma) = \varphi$.

We shall now show, without complete proof by mathematical induction, that this linear bounded automaton simulates the derivations of G and only those of G. The states s_o and s_1 function to verify that a string of terminal elements is found between the two boundary symbols #. Rules 1 and 2 show that the automaton starting at the left-hand boundary symbol passes over all terminal elements until the right-hand boundary symbol is reached. Rule 3 indicates that at that point state t_o is reached. If symbols other than terminal elements are found between the boundary symbols, the machine blocks and the string is not accepted. Rules 4 through 7 see to it that the automaton can move freely to the left or to the right without altering the content of the input; it can simply write the symbol it reads. Rules 8 through 11 see to it that the automaton can transpose elements or pairs of elements only according to the productions in P. Rules 12 through 15 see to the correct inversion of productions $S \to SA$, the only rules in Kuroda normal-form in which S can appear to the right of the arrow. Because these are the only expanding productions in the grammar, it must be possible to derive the input string x in grammar G as $S \Rightarrow SA \Rightarrow SAA \Rightarrow \ldots \Rightarrow SA \ldots A \overset{*}{\Rightarrow} x$. This is simulated in reverse order by the linear bounded automaton by replacing $\#SAB\ldots\#$, where possible, with $\#\#SB\ldots\#$. This can occur because when the automaton in the "work-state" t_o reads S, it changes to state r_o (rule 12) and moves one place to the left to see if there is an S next to the boundary symbol #. If that is the case, the automaton changes to state r_1 and, provided that $S \rightarrow SA$ is a production of P, rules 14 and 15 replace SA with $\#S$, and the work-state t_0 is again reached. The automaton then sees if SB can be reduced to S; if it is, $\#\#\#S...\#$ appears on the tape, and the process continues. In this way the string $\#\# ... \#S\#$ will appear on the tape only if x can be derived from S. Once the automaton has reached state t_0, rules 12, 13, and 14[1] see to it that it goes on to state t_1 and proceeds to the right in order to read the last boundary symbol. According to rule 16, when the automaton reaches the final state s_0 and the tape is pushed out, string x is accepted.

If we wish to have LBA also accept the null-string λ, we must add a new state t_λ, and two new transition rules: $\delta(t_0, \#)$ contains $(t_\lambda, \#, 1)$, and $(t_\lambda, \#)$ contains $(s_0, \#, 1)$. With these, when the input is λ, the final state is reached immediately after completion of the steps required by rules 1, 2, and 3.

EXAMPLE 6.2. Take grammar $G = (V_N, V_T, P, S)$, with $V_N = \{S, A, B\}$, $V_T = \{a, b\}$, and the following productions:

(a) $S \rightarrow SA$ (d) $A \rightarrow a$
(b) $S \rightarrow B$ (e) $B \rightarrow b$
(c) $BA \rightarrow AB$

Because of production (c) it is clear that grammar G is context-sensitive and that it is in Kuroda normal-form. G generates the language $L(G) = \{a^iba^j \mid i + j \geqslant 0\}$. The sentences are thus strings of a's with one b in them. Production (a) generates the string SA^n; production (b) replaces the single S with B; by production (c) the B can be moved any number of places to the right. Productions (d) and (e) replace the variables with terminal symbols.

[1] Notice that rule 14 exists only if there is indeed a production $S \rightarrow SA$ in P. If this were not the case, the operation would stop. When no such production exists, language $L(G)$ consists exclusively of sentences of length 1, and it obviously remains possible to construct a linear bounded automaton which accepts that language and only that language. Also rule 14 strictly violates the convention that no new boundary symbols may be written. Paragraph 7.1 gives an easy way out.

We can construct a linear bounded automaton *LBA* which accepts $L(G)$, according to the procedure given in the proof of Theorem 6.1. Thus $LBA = (S, I, \Gamma, \delta, s_0, \#, F)$, with $S = \{s_0, s_1, t_0, t_1, t_B, r_0, r_1\}$, $I = \{a, b\}$, $\Gamma = \{S, A, B, a, b, \#\}$, $F = \{s_0\}$, and the following transition rules in δ:

1. $\delta(s_0, \#) = \{(s_1, \#, 1)\}$
2. $\delta(s_1, a) = \{(s_1, a, 1)\}$ because $a \in V_T$
3. $\delta(s_1, b) = \{(s_1, b, 1)\}$ because $b \in V_T$
4. $\delta(s_1, \#) = \{(t_0, \#, -1)\}$
5. $\delta(t_0, S) = \{(t_0, S, 1), (t_0, S, -1), (r_0, S, -1)\}$ because $S \in V_N$
6. $\delta(t_0, A) = \{(t_0, A, 1), (t_0, A, -1), (t_B, B, 1)\}$ because $A \in V_N$, and $BA \rightarrow AB$ in P
7. $\delta(t_0, B) = \{(t_0, B, 1), (t_0, B, -1), (t_0, S, 0)\}$ because $B \in V_N$, and $S \rightarrow B$ in P
8. $\delta(t_0, a) = \{(t_0, a, 1), (t_0, a, -1), (t_0, A, 0)\}$ because $a \in V_T$, and $A \rightarrow a$ in P
9. $\delta(t_0, b) = \{(t_0, b, 1), (t_0, b, -1), (t_0, B, 0)\}$ because $b \in V_T$, and $B \rightarrow b$ in P
10. $\delta(t_B, B) = \{(t_0, A, 0)\}$ because $BA \rightarrow AB$ in P
11. $\delta(r_0, \#) = \{(r_1, \#, 1)\}$
12. $\delta(r_1, S) = \{(t_1, \#, 1)\}$ $\Big\{$ because $S \rightarrow SA$ in P
13. $\delta(t_1, A) = \{(t_0, S, 0)\}$ $\Big\{$
14. $\delta(t_1, \#) = \{(s_0, \#, 1)\}$

The following shows the consecutive configurations in *LBA* for the acceptance of the sentence *abaa*; the numbers over the transition symbols $\vdash$ indicate the rule used in the transition.

$$s_0\#abaa\# \overset{1}{\vdash} \#s_1abaa\# \overset{2}{\vdash} \#as_1baa\# \overset{3}{\vdash} \#abs_1aa\# \overset{2}{\vdash} \#abas_1a\# \overset{2}{\vdash} \#abaas_1\# \overset{4}{\vdash} \#abat_0a\# \overset{8}{\vdash} \#abat_0A\# \overset{6}{\vdash} \#abt_0aA\# \overset{8}{\vdash} \#abt_0AA\# \overset{6}{\vdash} \#at_0bAA\# \overset{9}{\vdash} \#at_0BAA\# \overset{7}{\vdash} \#t_0aBAA\# \overset{8}{\vdash} \#t_0ABAA\# \overset{6}{\vdash} \#Bt_BBAA\# \overset{10}{\vdash} \#Bt_0AAA\# \overset{6}{\vdash} \#t_0BAAA\# \overset{7}{\vdash} \#t_0SAAA\# \overset{5}{\vdash} r_0\#SAAA\# \overset{11}{\vdash} \#r_1SAAA\# \overset{12}{\vdash} \#\#t_1AAA\# \overset{13}{\vdash} \#\#t_0SAA\# \overset{5,11,12,13}{\vdash} \#\#\#t_0SA\# \overset{5,11,12,13}{\vdash} \#\#\#\#t_0S\# \overset{5,11,12}{\vdash} \#\#\#\#\#t_1\# \overset{14}{\vdash} \#\#\#\#\#\#s_0.$$

To complete the statement of equivalence between linear bounded automata and context-sensitive grammars, we mention the following theorem.

THEOREM 6.2. For every linear bounded automaton *LBA*, there is a context-sensitive grammar G such that $T(LBA) = L(G)$.

A large number of rules are needed for the construction of such an equivalent context-sensitive grammar. The proof of this theorem is beyond the scope of this book; for it we refer the reader to Landweber (1963) and Kuroda (1964).

7

TURING MACHINES

An obvious question at this point is whether it is possible to design an automaton which could accept type-0 languages. The answer is affirmative; in fact some time before the theory of formal languages came into existence, Turing had described an automaton which later proved capable of accepting type-0 languages. The TURING MACHINE, as the automaton is called, is in principle capable of performing every operation which one might intuitively qualify as a MECHANICAL (EFFECTIVE)PROCEDURE (cf. paragraph 2.1.). In this chapter we will make the notion of "procedure" more explicit in order to facilitate an understanding of a number of important properties of natural languages. However, we shall first show that Turing machines accept type-0 languages and only type-0 languages, and that there exists a type-0 grammar for every language accepted by a Turing machine.

In this chapter, more than in the preceding chapters, theorems will be stated without proof. The theory of Turing machines has recourse to refined fields of mathematics, such as recursive function theory, with which we can suppose no acquaintance on the part of the reader. Moreover Turing machines are less of interest to linguistics and psycholinguistics than automata of more limited capacity. Therefore, we shall state and discuss only a limited number of theorems which are of some importance to linguistics.

7.1. DEFINITIONS AND CONCEPTS

Several different but equivalent terminologies have been used in describing Turing machines. The terminology which we shall use here is closely akin to that of linear bounded automata used in the preceding chapter

Like linear bounded automata, a Turing machine is made up of a finite automaton and a tape. A Turing machine can read and write tape symbols in the same way as a linear bounded automaton, but it is not subject to linear limitation: it can read and write to the left and to the right of the original input. We must suppose that the length of the tape is infinite, and that at the beginning of an operation a limited and continuous portion of the tape carries input symbols, bordered left and right by boundary symbols. To facilitate further formulation, we also suppose that the remainder of the tape is filled with boundary symbols. The machine can read the boundary symbols and replace them with other tape symbols, but cannot itself write boundary symbols. Consequently the tape carries a continuous string of input symbols which cannot be interrupted by boundary symbols. On the other hand, there may be "pseudo-boundary symbols", equivalent in every respect to the ordinary boundary symbols except in that they may also be written; in informal treatment of Turing machines, the distinction between the two types of boundary symbols is often neglected.

The notation will be the same as that used for linear bounded automata.

In formal terms, a Turing machine TM is a system $(S, I, \Gamma, \delta, s_0, \#, F)$, in which:

(1) S is a finite set of STATES, with s_0 as the INITIAL STATE, and $F \subset S$ as the set of FINAL STATES.

(2) I is a finite set of INPUT SYMBOLS.

(3) Γ is a finite set of TAPE SYMBOLS, of which I is a subset. Elements of Γ which are not elements of I are called AUXILIARY SYMBOLS, one of which is the BONUDARY SYMBOL $\#$. In the initial configuration the tape carries a string from I^*, bordered on the left and on the right by strings of boundary symbols of infinite length.

(4) δ is a finite set of TRANSITION RULES which indicate, for every pair of state and input symbol, what the machine must write (the boundary symbol cannot be written by the machine), what the following state will be, and whether the machine will remain at the same place on the tape, or move one step to the left or right. It is also possible for the machine to block. We can therefore say that δ maps $S \times \Gamma$ in $S \times \{\Gamma - \#\} \times \{-1, 0, 1\} \cup \varphi$. The transition rules have the form $\delta(s, \gamma) = (s', \gamma', k)$, where $k = -1$, 0, or 1. They should be interpreted as follows: if the Turing machine is in state s and reads the symbol γ, it passes to state s', writes γ' over the symbol γ, and moves the tape according to the value of k. Turing machines are deterministic; for every combination of state and tape symbol, only one transition is possible. It is possible, of course, to define nondeterministic Turing machines, but these are equivalent to deterministic Turing machines.[1] (We shall use nondeterministic Turing machines in the proof of Theorem 7.1.).

Before defining the language accepted by a Turing machine, we must indicate what is meant here by configuration. As was the case for linear bounded automata, a configuration in a Turing machine includes the content of the tape, the state of the automaton, and the position of the tape content in relation to the automaton. The notation is the same as for configurations in linear bounded automata, but redundant boundary symbols are omitted. Thus, for example, $s\#\gamma_1\gamma_2 \ldots \gamma_n\#$ stands for $\ldots\#\#s\#\gamma_1\gamma_2 \ldots \gamma_n\#\#\#\ldots$, and means that the Turing machine is in state s and is reading the boundary symbol directly to the left of the tape content $\gamma_1\gamma_2 \ldots \gamma_n$. The initial configuration is $s_0\#w\#$, where $w \in I^*$. A final configuration is every configuration in which the Turing machine is in a final state: $\omega s_f \chi$, where ω and χ are elements of Γ^*, and s_f is an element of F. In this case the automaton is said to STOP (stopping should not be confused with blocking). A string x in I^* is accepted by a Turing machine when $s_o\#x\# \vdash^* \omega s_f \chi$. The LANGUAGE accepted by a Turing machine is the set of the strings in I^* accepted by the machine. Figure 7.1. illustrates an initial

[1] It is not known whether deterministic and nondeterministic linear bounded automata are also equivalent.

configuration, a configuration during operation, and a final configuration of a Turing machine in the process of accepting the input string $x = a_1 \dots a_m$.

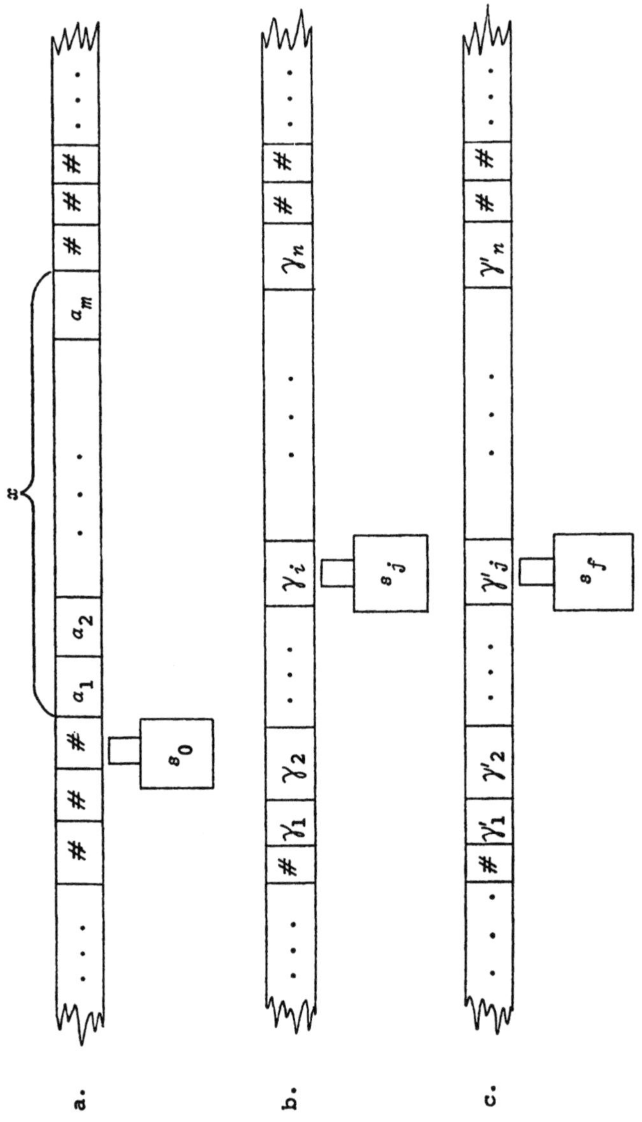

Fig. 7.1. A Turing Machine in Operation a. Initial configuration.
b. The machine in operation.
c. Final configuration.

7.2. A FEW ELEMENTARY PROCEDURES

In this paragraph we shall give a few examples of operations which can be performed by a Turing machine. The operations given here will later serve as elementary procedures in the comparison of Turing machines and type-0 grammars.

EXAMPLE 7.1. The transfer of information on the tape
In several cases it is necessary to transfer parts of the original input, or of the tape content which develops later, to a different place on the tape. In this way information can be stored while other operations are carried out. A simple example of this may be seen in the following Turing machine:

$TM = (S, I, \Gamma, \delta, s_o, \#, F)$, with $S = \{s_o, s_A, s_B, s_1, s_2, s_3\}$, $I = \{a, b\}$, $\Gamma = \{\#, a, b, c, A, B\}$, $F = \{s_3\}$, and where δ contains te following transition rules:

1. $\delta(s_o, \#) = (s_o, \#, 1)$	13 $\delta(s_B, A) = (s_B, A, 1)$
2. $\delta(s_o, a) = (s_A, c, 1)$	14. $\delta(s_B, B) = (s_B, B, 1)$
3. $\delta(s_o, b) = (s_B, c, 1)$	15. $\delta(s_B, \#) = (s_1, B, -1)$
4. $\delta(s_o, A) = (s_2, a, 1)$	16. $\delta(s_1, a) = (s_1, a, -1)$
5. $\delta(s_o, B) = (s_2, b, 1)$	17. $\delta(s_1, b) = (s_1, b, -1)$
6. $\delta(s_A, a) = (s_A, a, 1)$	18. $\delta(s_1, c) = (s_o, c, 1)$
7. $\delta(s_A, b) = (s_A, b, 1)$	19. $\delta(s_1, A) = (s_1, A, -1)$
8. $\delta(s_A, A) = (s_A, A, 1)$	20. $\delta(s_1, B) = (s_1, B, -1)$
9. $\delta(s_A, B) = (s_A, B, 1)$	21. $\delta(s_2, A) = (s_2, a, 1)$
10. $\delta(s_A, \#) = (s_1, A, -1)$	22. $\delta(s_2, B) = (s_2, b, 1)$
11. $\delta(s_B, a) = (s_B, a, 1)$	23. $\delta(s_2, \#) = (s_3, \#, 0)$
12. $\delta(s_B, b) = (s_B, b, 1)$	$\delta(-, -, -) = \varphi$ in all other cases.

This Turing machine will replace every string x in I^+, where $|x| = n$, with a string $c^n x$; the original string of a's and b's is moved exactly its length to the right and is replaced by a string of c's whose length is equal to that of the string of a's and b's. Let us take for example the transfer of the string aab. The following gives the successive configurations in the machine; the number of the transition rule involved is given over the transition symbol, except where a sequence of operations is repeated, in which case an asterisk * appears over the transition symbol.

$s_0\#aab\# \overset{1}{\vdash} \#s_0aab\# \overset{2}{\vdash} \#cs_Aab\# \overset{6}{\vdash} \#cas_Ab\# \overset{7}{\vdash} \#cabs_A\# \overset{10}{\vdash} \#cas_1bA\# \overset{17}{\vdash} \#cs_1abA\# \overset{16}{\vdash} \#s_1cabA\# \overset{18}{\vdash} \#cs_0abA\# \overset{2}{\vdash} \#ccs_AbA\# \overset{*}{\vdash} \#ccbs_1AA\# \overset{19}{\vdash} \#ccs_1bAA\# \overset{17}{\vdash} \#cs_1cbAA\# \overset{18}{\vdash} \#ccs_0bAA\# \overset{3}{\vdash} \#cccs_BAA\# \overset{*}{\vdash} \#cccAAs_B\# \overset{15}{\vdash} \#cccAs_1AB\# \overset{*}{\vdash} \#cccs_0AAB\# \overset{4}{\vdash} \#cccas_2AB\# \overset{21}{\vdash} \#cccaas_2B\# \overset{22}{\vdash} \#cccaabs_2\# \overset{23}{\vdash} \#cccaabs_3\#.$

EXAMPLE 7.2. The comparison of two strings
At times it is necessary to decide whether two strings of elements are identical. One can easily see that this is possible with a Turing machine. Imagine that we are interested in two strings r_1 and r_2 over a vocabulary V. We place the string r_1cr_2 on the tape, where $c \notin V$. The language $T = wcw$ is then a context-sensitive language with a vocabulary $V \cup \{c\}$. This means that there is a context-sensitive grammar which generates the sentences wcw and only the sentences wcw. There is consequently a linear bounded automaton *LBA* which accepts language T, and since Turing machines are a generalization of the linear bounded automaton, there is a Turing machine which accepts language T. In other words, a Turing machine accepts a string r_1cr_2 on condition that $r_1 = r_2$, and can therefore be considered an automaton which determines the identity of two strings.

7.3. TURING MACHINES AND TYPE-0 LANGUAGES

It is possible to construct a "Universal Turing machine" *UTM*, which can simulate the operation of any given Turing machine. A description of the *TM* (its transition rules, etc.) would be placed on the input tape of the *UTM*, while the input of the *TM* would appear in another place on the input tape of the *UTM*. Thus "programmed", the *UTM* would imitate the operation of the *TM* precisely. It is even possible to construct a *UTM* with only two states, but it would need an extremely large tape vocabulary.

However, it is not our intention to discuss Universal Turing machines here. We have mentioned them only to render the proposition acceptable that various elementary procedures for which Turing machines have been constructed can be combined in a single Turing machine. Such a machine could switch over from one procedure to another, just as a digital computer can switch from one subroutine to another. (The only essential difference between a computer and a Turing machine is that the latter disposes of an unlimited store: all information presented can be stored on a tape of infinite length.) With this background, we can discuss the following theorem.

THEOREM 7.1. For every type-0 language L there is a Turing machine such that $T(TM) = L$.

PROOF (summary). The construction of a TM which accepts language L is roughly as follows. Let L be a type-0 language, and G the type-0 grammar which generates it. Let x be a sentence in L. We put the string x on the input tape as $\#x\#$, and build in a procedure according to which the symbols c and S (neither of which are elements of V_T) are added to the string as follows: $\#xcS\#$. For every production $\alpha \rightarrow \beta$ in G we construct such transition rules for TM that a string α can be rewritten on the tape as β. If α is not of the same length as β, it will be necessary at rewriting to transfer the information directly to the right of α, either to the left or to the right, so that β will fit precisely into place. Therefore we must include a transfer procedure in the Turing machine, similar to that of Example 7.2.

TM can nondeterministically replace S with some β, where $S \rightarrow \beta$ is a production in G. Let $\beta = B_1 B_2 \dots B_n$ (where B_i is an element of V, but not necessarily of V_N). In that case the tape shows $\#xcB_1B_2 \dots B_n\#$.

Next we must build a procedure into TM according to which the left-hand members (α_i) of the productions $\alpha_1 \rightarrow \beta_i$ can be rewritten as an identification symbol. The automaton now nondeterministically chooses an α_i and a B_j from the string mentioned above, and switches over to a comparison procedure which compares α_i element for element with $B_j B_{j+1}$ .... Example 7.2. showed that such a comparison procedure is possible in principle. If string α_i is identical to string $B_j B_{j+1}$ ..., it is replaced by β_i, the right-hand member of the production $\alpha_i \to \beta_i$. By continued replacement of strings between c and # according to the productions of G, a string of terminal elements is (nondeterministically) composed between c and #. At this point the Turing machine can switch back to the comparison procedure in order to compare this new string with string x. If the two are identical, the machine reaches a final state and stops. It is clear that the terminal strings between c and # can only be sentences of $L(G)$, and that any sentence in $L(G)$ can appear there. Thus TM accepts the sentences of $L(G)$ and only the sentences of $L(G)$. If there is a nondeterministic Turing machine which accepts $L(G)$ and only $L(G)$, then there is a deterministic Turing machine which does the same.

THEOREM 7.2. For every language T accepted by a TM, there is a type-0 grammar G such that $L(G) = T(TM)$.

PROOF (summary). Let T be the language accepted by Turing machine TM. For every x in T, TM goes from its initial state to a final state in a finite number of operations: $s_o\#x\# \vdash^* \#\omega s_f \chi\#$, with $s_f \in$ F and $\omega, \chi \in \Gamma^*$. We write x as $a_1 a_2 \ldots a_n$ $(n > 0)$. The first step in the process of accepting is as follows: $s_o\#a_1a_2...a_n\# \vdash \#s_o a_1 a_2 ... a_n\#$. Another transition arbitrarily chosen is $\#\psi\gamma_1 s\gamma_2\sigma\# \vdash \#\psi s'\gamma_1\gamma_2'\sigma\#$ if TM moves to the left (with s, $s' \in S$, γ_1, $\gamma_2, \gamma_2' \in \Gamma$, and $\psi, \sigma \in \Gamma^*$). This can be described as rewriting triads:

(1) $\gamma_1 s\gamma_2 \to s'\gamma_1\gamma_2'$.

Nothing else changes in the configuration, and given the construction of TM, the transition is completely determined by the triad $\gamma_1 s\gamma_2$. There is a similar pair of triads for the case that the machine moves to the right. The transition has the form $\#\psi s\gamma_1\gamma_2\sigma\# \vdash \#\psi\gamma_1' s'\gamma_2\sigma\#$ and can be represented as a rewrite:

(2) $s\gamma_1\gamma_2 \to \gamma_1' s'\gamma_2$.

If the machine remains in place, we write:

(3) $s\gamma_2 \rightarrow s'\gamma'_2$.

Because the number of states s and tape symbols γ for each Turing machine is finite, the number of pairs or triads is also finite. A subset of the set of these pairs gives a complete description of the possible operations of the Turing machine. Because Turing machines are deterministic, for every triad or pair to the left of the arrow there is only one possible triad or pair which can follow to the right of the arrow. Therefore, we can conclude that the operation of every Turing machine can be completely described by means of a finite set of deterministic rewrite rules.

Let TM accept x. We have seen that the final configuration has the form $\#\omega s_f \chi\#$. It is not difficult to construct a Turing machine TM' equivalent to TM, which has as final configuration $\# s_f S' \#$. For this purpose we build TM' in such a way that, just before reaching a final configuration, it will follow a procedure to replace all the remaining tape symbols with (pseudo) boundary symbols, except the last which is replaced by the as yet unused tape symbol S'. The initial and final configurations are therefore respectively $s_0\#x\#$ and $\#s_f S'\#$.

We can now construct a grammar G for which $L(G) = T(TM) = T(TM')$. We collect all the rules of types (1), (2), and (3) in TM'. If $\beta \rightarrow \alpha$ is a rule of TM', we make $\alpha \rightarrow \beta$ a production of G. Given the deterministic character of rules $\beta \rightarrow \alpha$, if $\alpha \rightarrow \beta$ and $\alpha' \rightarrow \beta$, then $\alpha = \alpha'$. Next we add to the productions of G the productions $S \rightarrow s_f S'$ for every s_f in F, and the production $s_0\# \rightarrow \#$. It is clear that by means of these productions, the derivations $S \Rightarrow s_f S' \overset{*}{\Rightarrow} x$ and only these can be made for every x in T and only if $x \in T$. G is a type-0 grammar, and consequently the theorem is proven.

It follows from Theorems 7.1. and 7.2. that Turing machines are equivalent to type-0 grammars or unrestricted rewrite systems.

7.4. MECHANICAL PROCEDURES, RECURSIVE ENUMERABILITY, AND RECURSIVENESS

Given a type-0 grammar G with a vocabulary V_T, there is a Turing machine TM which will stop in a final state after a finite number of transitions for every string x in V_T^* where $x \in L(G)$. We call this a mechanical procedure. In general we can define a mechanical (effective) procedure as an operation which can be performed by a Turing machine in a finite number of steps. Thus we replace the temporary definition of "procedure" given in paragraph 2.1. with the more precise definition "that which can be performed by means of a Turing machine". In paragraph 2.1. we imagined a procedure as a computer program by which an operation can be performed systematically. It does not at first seem evident that anything that can be performed systematically in a mechanical way (that is, without the use of human intuition), possibly by computer, can also be done on a Turing machine. The Turing machine appears to be far too simple a mechanism. But since the publication of Turing's original article (1936) it has become increasingly evident that the Turing machine can indeed perform anything which we might intuitively qualify as a procedure. For a good survey of the question, see Minsky (1967). It is therefore clearly justified formally to define the concept "procedure", as we have done, in terms of Turing machines. This opens the possibility of establishing with exactitude the problems for which no procedure exists, for such are the problems for which no Turing machine can be constructed. In the remainder of this chapter we shall speak freely of Turing machines whenever it is clear that a mechanical procedure must exist. Whenever we can explicitly indicate the consecutive steps of an operation, we conclude that the operation can be performed on a Turing machine.

The acceptance of a sentence by a Turing machine is by definition a mechanical procedure, but the same is true of the acceptance of sentences by more limited automata. It follows from the hierarchy of languages that for every language which is accepted by a finite automaton, a nondeterministic push-down automaton, or a linear bounded automaton, there exists a Turing machine which also accepts it. We can therefore treat the acceptance of languages and sentences by automata in general in terms of procedures.

We would point out that the definition of "accepting" has been rather weak for all automata. We know that if $x \in L$, there is a procedure (*TM*) which will confirm that x is an element of L. But what happens if a string in V_T^* which is not an element of L is introduced as input? The Turing machine cannot reach a final state, but rather becomes blocked or goes on endlessly computing. We shall return to this point, but we shall first show that for every type-0 language L there is a mechanical procedure by which each sentence in L can be enumerated within a finite amount of time. L is then said to be RECURSIVELY ENUMERABLE.

THEOREM 7.3. Every type-0 language is recursively enumerable.

PROOF. It is easy to see that the strings in V_T^* can be enumerated by means of a mechanical procedure. If V_T contains k elements, the strings of V_T^* can be considered as numbers in a system with a base k, plus the null-string. If, for example, there are ten elements in V_T, we can give them the labels 0, 1, 2, ..., 9. strings of V_T^+ are thus numbers of the decimal system: 0, 1, 2, ..., 10, 11, ..., 100, 101, ..., and it is certainly possible to design a Turing machine which will write these sentences in sequence on its tape (the Turing machine must be able to perform the operation $n+1$). Each of these numbers appears on the tape after a finite number of operations, and no number is omitted. The same will hold for k. Furthermore, we know that there is a procedure which can determine whether a string is an element of L (Theorem 7.1.). This procedure can be applied to every newly enumerated string of V_T^*, in order to enumerate the sentences of L. There is a problem, however, for we do not know what will occur if the string in question is not an element of L. It is possible that the machine will go on endlessly computing and will never come to enumerate and test the following strings. This situation can be avoided by interrupting the test procedure at a given moment in the following way. We number the strings in V_T^*: $\lambda = 1$, $a_1 = 2$, $a_2 = 3$, etc. (this is possible, as we have seen), and we indicate by number how many transitions the *TM* can undergo at a given stage of the test procedure for a given string. The process takes place as shown in Table 7.1. In

TABLE 7.1. Test Procedure for the Enumeration of the Sentences of *L*.

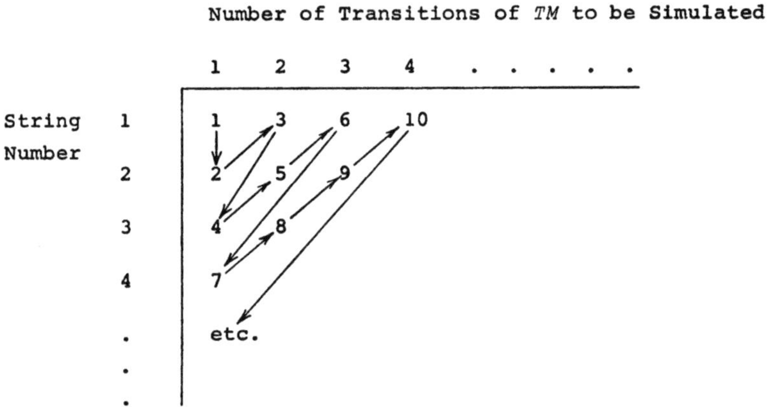

fact we have constructed a new Turing machine, *TM'*, which simulates the test procedure of *TM*. *TM'* first tests string 1 to see if it is an element of *L* by simulating one transition of the procedure of *TM*. If *TM'* finds that the string is an element of *L*, it enumerates the string and proceeds to test string 2. If it is not yet clear whether or not string 1 is an element of *L*, *TM'* still proceeds to test string 2. According to the table, *TM'* may simulate again only one transition of *TM*. String 2 is or is not enumerated according to the results of this test; according to the table, *TM'* then goes back to string 1 and simulates two steps from *TM* to test the string. According to the results of this test, the string is or is not enumerated, and *TM'* then goes on to test string 3 with one step from *TM*. It goes on in the same way to test string 2 with two transitions, string 1 with three transitions, string 4 with one transition, and so forth. In this way the automaton returns to each string and performs one step more than the preceding time to test it. Thus each string in

V_T^* is successively tested for membership in L by way of a finite number of transitions. For each x in L the procedure finally leads to the acceptance and enumeration of x.

We state without proof that the inverse of Theorem 7.3. is also valid: every recursively enumerable language can be generated by a type-0 grammar.

We have seen that the recursive enumerability of a type-0 language follows from the existence of an accepting procedure for the sentences of L, and have remarked that this is a weak theorem. We do not know what the Turing machine will do to a string in V_T^* which does not belong to the language. In order to discuss this question further, we define the COMPLEMENT OF A LANGUAGE L, with vocabulary V_T, as $V_T^* - L$. This is the set of strings over the terminal vocabulary which are not elements of the language. Linguists call this the set of UNGRAMMATICAL SENTENCES. The complement of a language is denoted by CL.

A stronger form of acceptance would be a procedure according to which for every string in V_T^* it would be indicated if the string belongs to L or to CL. One might imagine a "twin Turing machine" which would reach a final state for a string in CL, while the original Turing machine would do the same for a string in L. One might also imagine a Turing machine with two sets of final states, one for accepting, the other for rejecting. For every string x in V_T^*, the Turing machine would reach a final state: the accepting final state when $x \in L$, and the rejecting final state when $x \in CL$. If such a procedure exists for language L, the automaton is said to RECOGNIZE (as opposed to accept) L. A recognition procedure of this sort is usually called an ALGORITHM. An algorithm is thus a procedure according to which for every x in V_T^*, it can be determined whether or not x belongs to L. Because algorithms lead to decisions for every string in V_T^*, the language $L \subset V_T^*$ is called a DECIDABLE (RECURSIVE) SET if an algorithm exists for the recognition of L. It follows from the construction of the twin Turing machines that a language is recursive if both the language and its complement are recursively enumerable.

We know that type-0 languages, and consequently also type-1, type-2, and type-3 languages are recursively enumerable, but are the complements of these languages also recursively enumerable? That is not the case in general. We state without proof that there are type-0 languages which are not recursive, because they have complements which are not recursively enumerable. This means that the complements are not type-0 languages. However, the complement of a context-sensitive language is recursively enumerable, and consequently context-sensitive; context-free and regular languages are all recursive. There are (recognition) algorithms for all of these languages.

We have seen that the complement of a type-0 language is not necessarily itself of type-0, but what of the other language types? It is not yet known if the complement of a context-sensitive language is context-sensitive; all we know is that it is recursively enumerable, and consequently of type-0. It has been proven that no general procedure exists for determining whether the complement of any context-free language is also context-free. In any case it does not hold in general that the complement of a context-free language is also context-free; the complement of a deterministic context-free language is, however, also deterministic and context-free. It is also known that the complement of a regular language is likewise regular.

8

GRAMMATICAL INFERENCE

8.1. HYPOTHESES, OBSERVATIONS, AND EVALUATION

Is it possible on the basis of samples of a language to decide on an acceptable grammar for that language? In its present form, this question cannot be answered, but the day to day work of the linguist, as well as the fast growing language capacity of the young child, suggest that an affirmative answer might be expected to at least some forms of the question. The answer depends on (1) what is known about the grammar, (2) the composition of the sample of data, and (3) what is understood by "acceptable". The investigation of these matters is known as the study of GRAMMATICAL INFERENCE.

That which is already known or supposed of a grammar is referred to by the term HYPOTHESIS-SPACE. The terminal vocabulary V_T, for instance, is ordinarily given. Certain suppositions can also be made as to the class to which the grammar belongs (regular, context-free, etc.). In the case of a probabilistic grammar, not only can suppositions be made about the type of grammar, but inference can also have the more limited goal of finding the most acceptable production probabilities for a grammar which is given. This latter has rather direct possibilities of application, and we will deal with it in some detail in paragraph 8.2. Paragraph 8.3. will treat a number of general findings relative to nonprobabilistic hypothesis-space, and paragraph 8.4. will discuss the most general kind of hypothesis-space, probabilistic grammars for which both productions and production probabilities must be found.

The term OBSERVATION-SPACE refers to the composition of the data sample; it can take on various forms. If L is the language investigated and x is a given string in V_T^*, we can obtain positive information, $x \in L$, or negative information, $x \notin L$ (i.e. $x \in CL$), about L. In the former case we speak of a POSITIVE INSTANCE, in the latter, of a NEGATIVE INSTANCE. The information available is called an INFORMATION SEQUENCE. If all the instances in the sequence are positive, we have a POSITIVE INFORMATION SEQUENCE; if negative instances also occur, we have a MIXED INFORMATION SEQUENCE. A COMPLETE INFORMATION SEQUENCE is a mixed information sequence in which all positive and negative instances are enumerated; such sequences are generally infinite in length. A COMPLETE POSITIVE INFORMATION SEQUENCE is the enumeration of all positive instances; it is called TEXT PRESENTATION, since the language is presented, sentence for sentence, as a text. Repetitions may occur, provided that the enumeration is complete, i.e. every sentence of the language must occur after a finite number of other sentences. INFORMANT PRESENTATION is the term for a complete mixed information sequence, or a sequence in which every positive and negative instance over V_T^* occurs after a finite number of other instances. One might picture this as a researcher who wishes to find the grammar of a language and reads each string of V_T^* to an informant who in turn tells him for every string whether it belongs to the language or not. A STOCHASTIC TEXT PRESENTATION is an infinite sequence $I = x_1, x_2, \ldots,$ where x_i is an element of L, and L is a probabilistic language in which for every x_i, $p(\underset{\sim}{x}_i = x_i) = p(\underset{\sim}{x} = x)$;[1] this means that the chance that string x will be in position i is constant and equal to the probability of the string in the language. The sentences thus appear successively with their respective probabilities in L. Notice that the definition of a stochastic text presentation does not include the property of completeness. At the limit, however, the relative frequency of a sentence in a stochastic text presentation is equal to its probability in L. The chance of occurrence of a sentence x in L can be increased by

[1] $p(\underset{\sim}{x} = x)$ is the probability of x in L. We suppose the variables x_i to be independent, i.e. $p(\underset{\sim}{x}_i = x_i \mid \underset{\sim}{x}_j = x_j) = p(\underset{\sim}{x}_i = x_i)$.

increasing the length of the information sequence. A sample of a stochastic text presentation of size k consists of the first k elements of that text presentation. On the basis of the assumption of independence,[2] the probability of this particular sample is the product of the probabilities of its k elements.

What is an "acceptable" grammar? Suppose that the information consists of an information sequence up to a given point k: x_1, x_2, ..., x_k. Any grammar which corresponds to the elements x_1, ..., x_k is, in a weak sense, acceptable. By "corresponds" we mean that the positive instances in the sequence are generated by the grammar, and the negative instances are not. But the criterion of correspondence will in general allow an infinity of possible grammars. If we concentrate our attention on the positive instances in the text presentation, we find that the one extreme is a grammar which generates only the k elements of the information, whereas the other extreme is a universal (regular) grammar over V_T which generates all the strings of V_T^*. Both these grammars correspond to the information, but the former is "unnecessarily" complex, and the latter would correspond to any sample, and therefore does not "fit". Both complexity and fit must decidedly be included in the standard of evaluation of the acceptability of a grammar. To a large extent, complexity is a matter of teste and of the preferences of the researcher. That the standard is relative is probably the only point on which one could expect all to agree. Grammars may be compared on the basis of various criteria, such as the number of symbols, the number of productions, the number of alternatives for each production, etc. These criteria make up the context of evaluation; on it depends the complexity of a grammar. The use of the mechanism of probabilistic grammars can permit a definition of context (without excluding other definitions, as complexity remains a matter of taste) in terms of the a priori probability of alternative grammars in the hypothesis-space. This will be done in paragraph 8.4; it will at the same time permit an evaluation, by way of the Bayes theorem, of the fit of various probabilistic grammars.

2 See note 1.

In the following paragraph, however, we shall deal only with the classical statistical evaluation procedure. This method is more efficient in that context, and yields results for large samples which scarcely deviate from those of a Bayes analysis.

8.2. THE CLASSICAL ESTIMATION OF PARAMETERS FOR PROBABILISTIC GRAMMARS

We will be dealing here with the simple case in which, except for the production probabilities, the entire grammar is given. The discussion will be limited to nonambiguous context-free grammars.

On the basis of a sample of language L, we must determine which probabilistic grammar will be the best for L, that is, we must find an optimal estimate for the production probabilities of the grammar.

Let G be a nonambiguous context-free grammar with N productions. The respective production probabilities are labelled p_1, p_2, ..., p_N. To normalize the grammar, we must see to it that for every variable A in V_N, $\sum_i p\ (A \rightarrow \alpha_1) = 1$. If there are $l(l > 0)$ productions in which A occurs to the left of the arrow, then for the productions $A \rightarrow \alpha_i$ (where $i = 1, 2, ..., l$), $l-1$ production probabilities must be found. (If G has only one production, $A \rightarrow x$, then $p(A \rightarrow x) = 1$.) If V_N has M variables, and the number of independent production probabilities in the grammar is denoted by k, then $k = N - M$. On the basis of the sample, estimates must be found for these k parameters, q_1, q_2, ..., q_k. When that is done, the production probabilities $p_1, p_2, ..., p_N$ will follow directly from the normalization.

Given a sample from language L, we proceed as follows. Let the sample contain n different sentences (or sentence types, since a particular sentence can occur more than once in the sample). The leftmost derivation $S \overset{*}{\Rightarrow} s_i$ must be determined for every sentence s_i (where $i = 1, ..., n$). If the productions used in the derivation are independent, then $p(S \overset{*}{\Rightarrow} s_i) = p(s_i)$ can be expressed as the product of the production probabilities p_i of the various steps in the derivation. For the derivation $S \overset{p_j}{\Rightarrow} \alpha \overset{p_k}{\Rightarrow} \beta \overset{p_l}{\Rightarrow} \gamma \overset{p_j}{\Rightarrow} s_i$, for example, this is $p(s_i) = p_j^2 p_k p_l$. This product for each of the n sentence types is denoted by π_i, and each of its terms can be expressed in parameters $q_1, \ldots, q_k$.

We define the likelihood function $\mathscr{L}$ for the sentences $s_i, \ldots, s_n$ and the parameters $q_1, \ldots, q_k$ as follows:

$$\mathscr{L}(s_1, \ldots, s_n; q_1, \ldots, q_k) = \pi_1^{f_1} \pi_2^{f_2} \ldots \pi_n^{f_n},$$

where f_i is the number of times sentence type i occurs in the sample. Using logarithms, this is:

$$\log \mathscr{L} = f_1 \log \pi_1 + f_2 \log \pi_2 + \ldots + f_n \log \pi_n = \sum_i f_i \log \pi_i.$$

The best estimate of the parameters $q_1, \ldots, q_k$ is that which gives a maximum for $\mathscr{L}$, and thus also for $\log \mathscr{L}$. With these parameters, the chance of drawing precisely this sample is at a maximum. The various parameter estimates $\hat{q}_1, \hat{q}_2, \ldots, \hat{q}_k$, are found by expressing every π_i in parameters, and then determining the k partial derivatives of $\mathscr{L}$ according to $q_1, \ldots, q_k$. This yields a system of k equations $\dfrac{\delta \log \mathscr{L}}{\delta q_i} = 0$, the solutions of which are the desired estimates $\hat{q}_1, \ldots, \hat{q}_k$. At this point the probabilities $p_1, \ldots, p_N$ can be calculated.

EXAMPLE 8.1. Let L be a language over the vocabulary $\{a, b, c\}$. Suppose we have a sample of L consisting of 100 sentences with the following distribution of sentence types: *c* (22 times), *aca* (42 times), *abcba* (19 times), *abbcbba* (12 times), *abbbcbbba* (4 times), and *abbbbcbbbba* (once). A possible grammar for these sentence types has the following productions:

$$S \overset{q_1}{\rightarrow} aAa \qquad\qquad A \overset{q_2}{\rightarrow} bAb$$

$$S \xrightarrow{1-q_1} c \qquad\qquad A \xrightarrow{1-q_2} c$$

Above the arrows we find the production probabilities expressed in parameters, and in such a way that the grammar is normalized. The leftmost derivations of the sentences in the sample are given below with the probability of the production concerned at each step.

$$S \overset{1-q_1}{\Longrightarrow} c \qquad p(c) = 1-q_1$$

$$S \overset{q_1}{\Rightarrow} aAa \overset{1-q_2}{\Longrightarrow} aca \qquad p(aca) = q_1(1-q_2)$$

$$S \overset{q_1}{\Rightarrow} aAa \overset{q_2}{\Rightarrow} abAba \overset{1-q_2}{\Longrightarrow} abcba \quad p(abcba) = q_1q_2(1-q_2)$$

etc.

$$p(abbcbba) = q_1q_2^2(1-q_2)$$

$$p(abbbcbbba) = q_1q_2^3(1-q_2)$$

$$p(abbbbcbbbba) = q_1q_2^4(1-q_2)$$

The likelihood function then becomes:

$\mathscr{L} = [(1-q_1)]^{22} [q_1(1-q_2)]^{42} [q_1q_2(1-q_2)]^{19} [q_1q_2^2(1-q_2)]^{12} \times [q_1q_2^3(1-q_2)]^4 [q_1q_2^4(1-q_2)] = q_1^{78}q_2^{59}(1-q_1)^{22}(1-q_2)^{78}$, and the natural logarithm of $\mathscr{L}$ is:

$\ln\mathscr{L} = 78 \ln q_1 + 59 \ln q_2 + 22 \ln (1-q_1) + 78 \ln (1-q_2)$. The most likely values of q_1 and q_2 are found by taking partial derivatives of $\ln\mathscr{L}$ with respect to q_1 and q_2, putting them equal to zero, and solving the equations:

$$\frac{\delta \ln\mathscr{L}}{\delta q_1} = \frac{78}{q_1} - \frac{22}{1-q_1} = 0 \qquad \frac{\delta \ln\mathscr{L}}{\delta q_2} = \frac{59}{q_2} - \frac{78}{1-q_2} = 0$$

thus $\hat{q}_1 = 0.78$ thus $\hat{q}_2 = 0.43$

With these estimates of the parameters, we can calculate the probabilities of the sentence types in the sample. For *c* we have $1\text{-}q_1 = 0.22$, for *aca*, $q_1(1\text{-}q_2) = 0.78 \times 0.57 = 0.445$, and so forth. In a sample of 100 sentences we would expect the sentence *c* 22 times, and the sentence *aca*, 44.5 times, etc. All the values are given in Table 8.1., together with the observed values. The correspondence between observed and expected values can be measured and evaluated with standard statistical tests such as, for example, the chi-square test for goodness of fit.

TABLE 8.1. Observed and Expected Frequencies of Sentence Types (Example 8.1.).

Sentence Type	Observed	Expected	Sentence Type	Observed	Expected
c	22	22	*abbbcbbba*	4	3.5
aca	42	44.5	*abbbbcbbbba*	1	1.5
abcba	19	19.1	other	0	1.2
abbcbba	12	8.2			

8.3. THE "LEARNABILITY" OF NONPROBABILISTIC LANGUAGES

A number of theorems concerning the "learnability" of non-probabilistic languages were presented by Gold in a fundamental article (1967). In this paragraph we shall state some of his more important findings without proving them.

Suppose we have a complete (text or informant) information sequence for a language of a given class (finite, regular, etc.). An algorithm must be found with the following characteristics:[1]
(1) each time a new input element x_t is introduced, the algorithm produces a grammar (or a code for a grammar) of the given class which is consistent with the information received up to that point.
(2) after a finite number of elements has been received, the output remains constant: the grammar produced as output is always the same or equivalent, and is a grammar of L.

A language is said to be IDENTIFIABLE IN THE LIMIT or LEARNABLE if such an algorithm exists for it for every complete information sequence. A class of languages is learnable if every language in it is learnable. The most important conclusions drawn by Gold from his investigation concerning the various classes of languages are given in Table 8.2.; in it, the symbol + denotes "learnable", and the symbol —, "not learnable".

[1] "Algorithm" is used in the same sense here as in the preceding chapter: a Turing machine which stops (produces an output) after every input. Gold also analyzes learnability as a procedure, but we will not discuss his findings here; they are not much different from the results for algorithms.

TABLE 8.2. "Learnability" of Languages of Various Classes according to Text or Informant Presentation

Language Class	Text	Informant
Type-0	—	—
Type-0 (recursive)	—	—
Type-0 (primitive recursive)	—	+
Context-Sensitive	—	+
Context-Free	—	+
Regular	—	+
Finite	+	+

The table calls for some explanation on (a) the broad difference between "learnabilty" on the basis of text presentation and "learnability" on the basis of informant presentation, and (b) the fine differentiation within the class of type-0 languages.

(a) Text presentation involves learnability for finite languages only. The fact that a finite language can be learned through text presentation can easily be understood as follows. Every sentence of the language appears after a finite number of earlier instances (since the presentation is complete). The algorithm can simply be to enumerate all different sentences which have appeared in the presentation up till and including the last instance. This list of sentences can as well be written as a grammar with rules $S \rightarrow x_i$ with one rule for every sentence x_i. After a finite amount of time, all the sentences of the language will have passed in review (as the number of sentences is finite), and from that point the grammar will remain unchanged. The grammar thus produced will certainly be a grammar of the language.

The process, however, will only succeed with finite languages; not even regular languages are learnable, according to Gold's definition of the term, on the basis of text presentation. One might imagine the following algorithm for the learning of regular languages on the basis of text presentation: the first and all following outputs of the algorithm would be a universal grammar U, with productions $S \rightarrow a$ and $S \rightarrow aS$ for every a in V_T. As such a grammar can generate any string in V_T^+, all subsequent outputs would be the same grammar, which will be consistent with all further information. But this algorithm would not satisfy condition (2) of the definition, because the grammar produced is not a grammar of the language (unless the language is the universal language V_T^+). The grammar would then be "too broad" for the language. The algorithm should be set up in such a way that the grammar is as narrow as possible at first, and is broadened according to the incoming information. As the class of finite languages is contained by the class of regular languages (Theorem 2.3.), it is not impossible that the language here in question be finite. The algorithm must begin here with the narrowest conjecture, namely that the language is finite. If it more broadly supposed the language to be infinite, while in fact the language was finite, it would never receive information incompatible with that supposition. We might, of course, imagine an algorithm which decides that a language is finite if it finds k repetitions of the same set of sentences, but this still would not solve the problem. Although such an algorithm would yield a correct grammar for a finite language, it could mistake an infinite for a finite language. Suppose, for example, that from infinite language L a text presentation is prepared as follows: take from L subsets F_1, F_2, ... of increasing size. Begin presenting the sentences in F_1 with k or more repetitions. The algorithm will then incorrectly decide that the language is finite. When F_2 is introduced, the algorithm must review its judgment, but if there are also k or more repetitions of the sentences in F_2, it will return to its original decision that the language is finite. But the same process will occur when F_3 is introduced, and so forth. The presentation is complete, for every sentence of the language will be presented after a finite amount of time, but the algorithm would always produce nothing other than grammars for finite languages. Thus an algorithm which functions flawlessly for finite languages cannot learn an infinite language, and an algorithm adapted to infinite languages will, when presented with a finite language, produce grammars which are too broad. Therefore it is impossible to "learn" an infinite language only on the basis of text presentation.

(b) In the preceding chapter it was stated that type-0 languages are generally not recursive. However there are type-0 languages which are recursive, but not context-sensitive; the set of recursive type-0 languages does not coincide completely with that of context-sensitive languages. The table shows that only "primitive recursive" type-0 languages, a subset of recursive type-0 languages, are learnable according to Gold's definition of the word. Primitive recursive languages cannot be defined without recourse to the theory of recursive functions.[1] Suffice it to note that "most" recursive languages are primitive recursive (also, in the history of mathematics, it has been difficult to find exceptions to this), and that the distinction between recursive and primitive recursive languages is of little importance to the study of natural languages. All recursive grammars (i.e. grammars of decidable languages) which will be mentioned below are in fact primitive recursive.

8.4. INFERENCE BY MEANS OF BAYES' THEOREM

In paragraph 8.2. we found by "classical" means optimal statistical parameters for a given nonambiguous context-free grammar. We renounced the possibility of choosing from among several grammars. In paragraph 8.3. the procedure was inverse, in a sense. We examined the conditions of presentation under which a grammar may be selected from the class of a priori possible grammars, renouncing the probabilistic formulation. The notion of "learnability" had to be defined in terms of equivalent grammars, as the algorithms cannot select an optimal or "most efficient" (cf. 3.1.) grammar from the class of equivalent adequate grammars.

Horning (1969) combined the two approaches, and developed a method of selecting an optimal probabilistic grammar from a

[1] A language is PRIMITIVE RECURSIVE if its characteristic function is primitive recursive. The characteristic function C_L of a language L, where $L \subset V_T^*$, has the value 1 for every string in V_T^* which is an element of L, and the value 0 for every string in V_T^* which is not an element of L.

Definitions of recursive functions may be found in Kleene (1952), Minsky (1967), Nelson (1968), *et alibi.*

given class on the basis of a given information sequence. We shall state some of his most important findings here concerning non-ambiguous context-free grammars.

We have seen that a standard of evaluation must express two aspects: the complexity of the grammar, and the degree to which it fits the information which is available at a given moment (paragraph 8.1.). The complexity of a grammar depends on the context, which includes at least (1) the size of the nonterminal vocabulary, (2) the number of alternative rewrites for a given variable, and (3) the length of those alternatives. (In practical and linguistic situations the context can include far more than this. The three aspects mentioned here, however, are constant themes in the linguistic literature on the subject.) The relative importance to be attributed to each of these aspects of context is a matter of taste, but there is a method by which this can at least be done in an exact manner. The method is by means of a so-called GRAMMAR-GRAMMAR. We will now introduce this notion.

A grammar is a finite string of symbols; a set of grammars (an hypothesis-space) may be regarded as a set of such strings, and thus as a kind of "language". A grammar-grammar is a grammar which generates such a "language". If the grammar-grammar is probabilistic, it will define a probability distribution over the "sentences" of the "language", and thus over the class of grammars which it generates. The complexity of a grammar can then be defined as minus the base two logarithm of its probability, as in information theory. The probabilistic grammar-grammar is thus a precise definition of the context; moreover, the more variables, the more alternatives for each variable, or the longer the alternatives in a generated grammar, the smaller its probability and the greater its complexity. The relative importance of each of the aspects can be varied by varying the production probabilities of the grammar-grammar.

We illustrate this with an example. To avoid confusion, name, variables, and arrow of the grammar-grammar are given in bold face type, while those of grammars are in ordinary type.

EXAMPLE 8.2. Let G be a probabilistic grammar-grammar with the following productions:

1. $\mathbf{S} \xrightarrow{0.5} \mathbf{R}$	7. $\mathbf{A} \xrightarrow{0.5} \mathbf{TN}$
2. $\mathbf{S} \xrightarrow{0.5} \mathbf{RR}$	8. $\mathbf{T} \xrightarrow{0.5} a$
3. $\mathbf{R} \xrightarrow{1} \mathbf{N} \rightarrow \mathbf{P}$	9. $\mathbf{T} \xrightarrow{0.5} b$
4. $\mathbf{P} \xrightarrow{0.5} \mathbf{A}$	10. $\mathbf{N} \xrightarrow{0.5} S$
5. $\mathbf{P} \xrightarrow{0.5} \mathbf{P}, \mathbf{A}$	11. $\mathbf{N} \xrightarrow{0.5} A$
6. $\mathbf{A} \xrightarrow{0.5} \mathbf{T}$	

This grammar-grammar generates regular grammars with one or two variables (S, A) and one or two terminal symbols (a, b). We shall show the leftmost derivation of a regular grammar G with the following productions:

$$S \rightarrow b, bS, aA \qquad\qquad A \rightarrow a, bA, aS$$

These are in fact six productions: the commas indicate alternative rewrites for a single variable. If we know that G is a context-free grammar, and thus that the first member of every production is a single variable, the grammar can be written without ambiguity as follows:

$$S \rightarrow b, bS, aAA \rightarrow a, bA, aS$$

(In the triad aAA, the reader should imagine a caesura between A and A.) This is precisely the "sentence" which we wish to derive from G; its leftmost derivation is as follows:

$\mathbf{S} \overset{0.5}{\Rightarrow} \mathbf{RR}$	$\overset{0.5}{\Rightarrow} \quad \rightarrow \mathbf{A}, \mathbf{A}, \mathbf{AR}$
$\overset{1}{\Rightarrow} \mathbf{N} \rightarrow \mathbf{PR}$	$\overset{0.5}{\Rightarrow} S \rightarrow \mathbf{T}, \mathbf{A}, \mathbf{AR}$
$\overset{0.5}{\Rightarrow} S \rightarrow \mathbf{PR}$	$\overset{0.5}{\Rightarrow} S \rightarrow b, \mathbf{A}, \mathbf{AR}$
$\overset{0.5}{\Rightarrow} S \rightarrow \mathbf{P}, \mathbf{AR}$	$\overset{0.5}{\Rightarrow} S \rightarrow b, \mathbf{TN}, \mathbf{AR}$
$\overset{0.5}{\Rightarrow} S \rightarrow \mathbf{P}, \mathbf{A}, \mathbf{AR}$	$\overset{0.5}{\Rightarrow} S \rightarrow b, b\mathbf{N}, \mathbf{AR}$

$$\overset{0.5}{\Rightarrow} S \rightarrow b,\ bS,\ \mathbf{AR}$$
$$\overset{0.5}{\Rightarrow} S \rightarrow b,\ bS,\ \mathbf{TNR}$$
$$\overset{0.5}{\Rightarrow} S \rightarrow b,\ bS,\ a\mathbf{NR}$$
$$\overset{0.5}{\Rightarrow} S \rightarrow b,\ bS,\ aA\mathbf{R}$$
$$\overset{1}{\Rightarrow} S \rightarrow b,\ bS,\ aA\mathbf{N} \rightarrow \mathbf{P}$$
$$\overset{0.5}{\Rightarrow} S \rightarrow b,\ bS,\ aAA \rightarrow \mathbf{P}$$
$$\overset{0.5}{\Rightarrow} S \rightarrow b,\ bS,\ aAA \rightarrow \mathbf{P},\ \mathbf{A}$$
$$\overset{0.5}{\Rightarrow} S \rightarrow b,\ bS,\ aAA \rightarrow \mathbf{P},\ \mathbf{A},\ \mathbf{A}$$
$$\overset{0.5}{\Rightarrow} S \rightarrow b,\ bS,\ aAA \rightarrow \mathbf{A},\ \mathbf{A},\ \mathbf{A}$$
$$\overset{0.5}{\Rightarrow} S \rightarrow b,\ bS,\ aAA \rightarrow \mathbf{T},\ \mathbf{A},\ \mathbf{A}$$
$$\overset{0.5}{\Rightarrow} S \rightarrow b,\ bS,\ aAA \rightarrow a,\ \mathbf{A},\ \mathbf{A}$$
$$\overset{0.5}{\Rightarrow} S \rightarrow b,\ bS,\ aAA \rightarrow a,\ \mathbf{TN},\ \mathbf{A}$$
$$\overset{0.5}{\Rightarrow} S \rightarrow b,\ bS,\ aAA \rightarrow a,\ b\mathbf{N},\ \mathbf{A}$$
$$\overset{0.5}{\Rightarrow} S \rightarrow b,\ bS,\ aAA \rightarrow a,\ bA,\ \mathbf{A}$$
$$\overset{0.5}{\Rightarrow} S \rightarrow b,\ bS,\ aAA \rightarrow a,\ bA,\ \mathbf{TN}$$
$$\overset{0.5}{\Rightarrow} S \rightarrow b,\ bS,\ aAA \rightarrow a,\ bA,\ a\mathbf{N}$$
$$\overset{0.5}{\Rightarrow} S \rightarrow b,\ bS,\ aAA \rightarrow a,\ bA,\ aS$$

The product of the probabilities of the rewrites is $p(G) = 0.5^{25}$, and the complexity of G in context $\mathbf{G}$ is thus $-{}^{2}\log 0.5^{25} = 25$. The reader can verify for himself that grammar U with productions $S \rightarrow a,\ b,\ aS,\ bS$ (this is the universal grammar which generates all strings in V_T^*) has a complexity of 15 in context $\mathbf{G}$.

If we consider it particularly important that a grammar should have few variables, we make production 2 less probable; the probability of a grammar with two variables decreases, and the complexity increases. If, on the other hand, we wish the number of alternative rewrites important, we can reduce the probability of production 5, which determines the number of alternatives for rewriting of a variable. Finally, if we wish to increase the importance of rewrite length, we reduce the probability of production 7. Many other variations are possible.[1]

We suppose that a complexity distribution is defined over the grammars in the hypothesis-space by means either of a grammar-

[1] One should, however, remain cautious. A grammar-grammar which generates all grammars of a certain type (e.g. regular grammars) will have a terminal vocabulary of infinite size, since the nonterminal vocabulary of every grammar generated is a subset of the terminal vocabulary of the grammar-grammar. Solutions to this problem have been found by Feldman, et al. (1969) and Horning (1969).

grammar or of some other context. We express the "credibility" of a grammar G_i in the hypothesis-space as a number $p(G_i)$, such that it is an inverse function of complexity (whichever way this is defined), with $0 < p(G_i) \leqslant 1$, and $\sum_i p(G_i) = 1$ for the grammars in the hypothesis-space. These propositions hold automatically in the context of a consistent probabilistic grammar-grammar. The p-values will be treated in all other regards as probabilities. We also suppose that the grammars in the hypothesis-space can be enumerated according to the order of their a priori credibility or "probability" p. (From this point we shall use the word "probability" exclusively.)

The observation-space is assumed to be a stochastic text presentation (cf. paragraph 8.1.).

As the OPTIMAL GRAMMAR we consider the a priori most probable grammar which is stochastically equivalent to the grammar by which the text was derived.

A procedure must be devised (in the sense of a Turing machine) which at receiving each new instance can maximalize the chance of conjecturing the optimal grammar, i.e. it must conjecture the grammar with the highest a posteriori probability, given the text and the a priori probabilities of the grammars. In order to investigate the existence of such a procedure we must, therefore, first explicate the relations between a priori and a posteriori probabilities of grammars.

The a priori probability of a grammar G_i in the hypothesis-space is denoted by $p(G_i)$. The probability of an information sequence (a sample) S_j, up to a given moment of the text presentation and given the hypothesis-space, is $p(S_j)$. The conditional probability that S_j will occur when G_i is really the grammar of the language is $p(S_j|G_i)$, and this is equal to the product of the probabilities of the sentences in the sample, given grammar G_i (cf. paragraph 8.1). Therefore, if the sample contains the sentences $s_1, s_2, \ldots, s_k$, then $p(S_j|G_i) = p(s_1|G_i) \cdot (p(s_2|G_i) \cdot \ldots \cdot p(s_k|G_i)$, or simply:

$$(1)\ p(S_j|G_i) = \prod_{j=1}^{k} p(s_j|G_i).$$

On the other hand we indicate the chance that G_i is really the grammar of L, given the sample S_j, as $p(G_i|S_j)$, which, according to an elementary rule of probability theory, is equal to $\frac{p(G_i, S_j)}{p(S_j)}$, where $p(G_i, S_j)$ is the chance that G_i is correct and that the sample S_j occurs. Therefore:

$$(2)\ p(G_i, S_j) = p(S_j) \cdot p(G_i|S_j).$$

This means that the common chance of G_i and S_j is the a priori probability of S_j, multiplied by the conditional probability that G_i is the real grammar when S_j occurs. For the sake of symmetry, this can also be written as follows:

$$(3)\ p(G_i, S_j) = p(G_i) \cdot p(S_j|G_i).$$

On the basis of (1) and (2) we can find the a posteriori probability of G_i:

$$(4)\ p(G_i|S_j) = \frac{p(G_i) \cdot p(S_j|G_i)}{p(S_j)}$$

(This is a form of the Bayes theorem.)

If we determine the a posteriori probabilities of all grammars in the hypothesis space, given the sample and the a priori probabilities, the denominator in (4), $p(S_j)$, remains constant, and only the two terms of the numerator vary. To find the optimal grammar, we must therefore find the grammar which yields the greatest numerator $p(G_i) \cdot p(S_j|G_i)$. We can write this product as $p'(G_i|S_j)$. If the sample contains k sentences, by substitution of (1) we get:

$$(5)\ p'(G_i|S_j) = p(G_i) \cdot \prod_{j=1}^{k} p(s_j|G_i).$$

Horning has proven that a procedure does exist by which at every new instance that G in the hypothesis-space can be found for which (5), and thus its posteriori probability, is at a maximum. We shall neither describe the procedure here nor prove the theorem, but only wonder if indeed the optimal grammar can, in the long run, be found in this way. In Gold's terms, the procedure does not lead, after a finite number of instances, to the reproduction at every new instance of the same grammar or stochastic equivalents which are grammars of the language. It only leads to the somewhat weaker result, that every nonoptimal grammar in the hypothesis-space is rejected after a finite number of instances. In other words, the chance that a nonoptimal grammar be conjectured decreases as the number of instances increases. This can also be regarded as a definition of "learnability", although it is weaker than that given by Gold. Taken in this sense, however, Horning has shown that probabilistic nonambiguous context-free grammars are "learnable" by means of a stochastic text presentation.

Until now we have assumed that the hypothesis-space consists of probabilistic grammars. However, if the hypothesis-space is generated by a probabilistic grammar-grammar this is not the case. Example 8.2. showed that the output of such a grammar-grammar is a grammar and its corresponding probability. Additionally, a way must be found to obtain optimal parameter estimates for production probabilities in the grammars in the hypothesis-space. Horning presents a (Bayes) procedure for this as well, and shows that the conclusions on learnability which we have just mentioned still hold in essence for this complete case.

HISTORICAL AND BIBLIOGRAPHICAL REMARKS

The theory of formal languages, except for the probabilistic part, is largely based on Chomsky's work. The original publication in which the hierarchy of grammars was introduced is Chomsky (1959 a, b.) A later survey is Chomsky (1963) in which the hierarchy of grammars was somewhat refined. Grammars with productions exclusively in the context-sensitive form were given a separate type number, and consequently the numeration differs there from that of the earlier work. We have followed current usage and maintained the original numeration.

The term "regular language" has a history of its own. Originally (Chomsky and Miller 1958; Bar-Hillel, Gaifman, and Shamir 1960) these languages were called "finite state languages" because of the connection with finite or finite state automata. But in mathematics, the theory of recursive functions dealt independently with, among other things, "regular sets", which can be recursively generated by "regular expressions", and Kleene showed the equivalence of these sets and the sets accepted by finite automata. As type-3 grammars are equivalent to finite automata (as in Theorems 4.2. and 4.3. proven by Chomsky and Miller 1958), type-3 languages are regular sets. Consequently type-3 grammars and languages are now generally called "regular grammars" and "regular languages".

Context-free grammars are treated in great detail in Chomsky's original work. The expression "normal-form" originated in Chomsky's notion of a "normal grammar" (Chomsky 1963). He said that normal grammars are the kind of grammars usually dealt with in linguistic discussions on constituent structure analysis: productions $A \to a$ concern the LEXICON of the language, and productions $A \to BC$ lead to binary divisions into CONSTITUENTS. At present, however, the term "normal-form" is used only to denote standardized forms for the productions of grammars. The Greibach normal-form is presented in Greibach (1965). The self-embedding theorem (Theorem 2.8.) for context-free languages was first formulated by Chomsky (1959a); a complete proof can be found in Salomaa (1969). The notion of ambiguity was first handled by Parikh (1961). For later developments see Ginsburg and Ullman (1966). For linear grammars see Greibach (1963) and (1966) and others. A textbook on context-free grammars is Ginsburg (1966).

The equivalence of type-1 grammars and grammars with productions only in the context-sensitive form was treated by Chomsky (1963). Grammars of the form which we have called the Kuroda normal-form were called "linear bounded grammars" by Kuroda and several other authors, by analogy with the automaton. The normal-form theorem (Theorem 2.11.) was first proven by Kuroda (1964).

The earliest publications on the subject of probabilistic grammars are Grenander (1967), Ellis (1969), and Booth (1969). It was an obvious matter to relate them to the Chomsky hierarchy. The consistency theorem for regular grammars (Theorem 3.1.) was proven by Ellis (1969) as was Theorem 3.2. The hypothesis formulated in Theorem 3.3. may be found in Suppes (1970). The Chomsky and Greibach normal-form theorems were originally proven by Ellis (1969); in the proof given here, we have followed Huang and Fu (1971). The conditions of consistency for probabilistic context-free grammars were investigated by Booth (1969) and Ellis (1969) where the reader may find more details on the subject.

The investigation of finite automata originated in the work of McCulloch and Pitts (1943), in which they gave models for neural networks which could be regarded as FINITE STATE MACHINES. Of the many early publications on this subject, we mention Rabin and Scott (1959), in which the proof of Theorem 4.1. can be found, and Kleene (1956). Later surveys are those by S. Ginsburg

(1962) and by A. Ginzburg (1968). The equivalence of finite automata and regular grammars (Theorems 4.2. and 4.3.) were proven by Chomsky and Miller (1958). Probabilistic finite automata were introduced by Rabin (1963). Much work in this area was done by Salomaa, who gives a good survey in Salomaa (1969).

The notion of the "push-down store" was introduced by Newell, Shaw, and Simon (1959). The first formulation of the relationship between push-down automata and formal languages is that of Oettinger (1961). The relationship between context-free grammars and push-down automata (Theorems 5.1. and 5.2.) was formulated by Chomsky (1963) and Evey (1963) more or less independently. The equivalence of deterministic push-down automata and $LR(k)$-grammars was proven by Knuth (1965).

Deterministic linear bounded automata were introduced by Myhill (1960); Landweber (1963) gave proof of Theorem 6.2. on deterministic linear bounded automata. Kuroda (1964) introduced the nondeterministic linear bounded automaton and proved the equivalence of them and context-free grammars (Theorems 6.1. and 6.2.).

The Turing machine was presented by Turing (1936) as a machine which could perform any computation for which an explicit procedure is known. For an introduction to the subject of mechanical (effective) procedures, see Minsky (1967); in the same work models by Post and Church, similar to the Turing machine, are also discussed. The relationship between Turing machines and type-0 languages formulated in Theorems 7.1. and 7.2. was first mentioned by Chomsky (1959a). We have borrowed the argumentation for Theorem 7.1. from Hopcroft and Ullman (1969). The argumentation for Theorem 7.2. was taken from Chomsky (1963), who in turn refers to Davis (1958), starting from the fact that type-0 languages are recursively enumerable sets. The argumentation for Theorem 7.3. was borrowed from Hopcroft and Ullman (1969). The first surveys of the relationship between formal languages and automata were Chomsky (1963) and Chomsky and Miller (1963) on the one hand, and Bar-Hillel (1964) on the other.

The earliest publication on grammatical inference is Miller and

Chomsky (1957). Solomonoff (1958, 1964 a, b) was the first to develop these ideas. The Feldman group, with among them Horning, has also done important work in this field (Feldman et al. 1969).

The best recent surveys of the subjects treated in this volume are Nelson (1968) where various topics are treated within the theory of formal systems, and Hopcroft and Ullman (1969) to which the present work is indebted and which would serve as excellent further reading. Neither of these books, however, deals with probabilistic grammars or probabilistic automata. For the latter, we refer the reader to Salomaa (1969). There are no standard texts on probabilistic grammars or grammatical inference.

BIBLIOGRAPHY

Bar-Hillel, Y.
1964 *Language and Information. Selected Essays on Theory and Application* (Reading, Mass.: Addison-Wesley).

Bar-Hillel, Y., C. Gaifman, and E. Shamir
1960 "On Categorical and Phrase Structure Grammars", *Bull. Res. Council of Israel* 9F: 1-16. (See also Bar-Hillel 1964.)

Booth, T. L.
1969 "Probability Representation of Formal Languages", *IEEE Tenth Annual Symposium on Switching and Automata Theory* (November).

Chomsky, N.
1959a "On Certain Formal Properties of Grammars", *Information and Control* 2: 137-67.
1959b "A Note on Phrase Structure Grammars", *Information and Control* 2: 393-95.
1962 "Context-Free Grammars and Pushdown Storage" (= *RLE Quart. Prog. Rept. No. 65*) (Cambridge, Mass.: MIT).
1963 "Formal Properties of Grammar", *Handbook of Mathematical Psychology*, R. D. Luce, R. R. Bush, and E. Galanter (eds.) (New York: Wiley).

Chomsky, N., and G. A. Miller
1958 "Finite State Languages", *Information and Control* 1: 91-112.
1963 "Introduction to the Formal Analysis of Natural Languages", *Handbook of Mathematical Psychology*, R. D. Luce, R. R. Bush, and E. Galanter (eds.) (New York: Wiley).

Chomsky, N., and M. P. Schützenberger
1963 "The Algebraic Theory of Context-free Languages", *Computer Programming and Formal Systems*, P. Braffort and D. Hirschberg (eds.) (Amsterdam: North-Holland).

Davis, Martin
1958 *Computability and Unsolvability* (New York: McGraw-Hill, 1958).

Ellis, G. A.
1969 "Probabilistic Languages and Automata" (= *Rept. no. 355. Dept. Comp. Sc.*) (University of Illinois, Urbana, Ill.).

Evey, R. J.
1963 "The Theory and Application of Pushdown Machines", *Mathematical*

Linguistics and Automatic Translation (= *Computation Lab. Rept.* NSF-10) (Cambridge, Mass.: Harvard).

Feldman, J. A., J. Gips, J. J. Horning, and S. Reder
1969 *Grammatical Complexity and Inference* (= *Techn. Rep. No. CS 125*) (Computer Science Dept., Stanford Univ.).

Feller, W.
1968 *An Introduction to Probability Theory and its Applications*, third edition (New York: Wiley).

Ginsburg, S.
1962 *An Introduction to Mathematical Machine Theory* (Reading, Mass.: Edison-Wesley).
1966 *The Mathematical Theory of Context-free Languages* (New York: McGraw-Hill).

Ginsburg, S., and J. Ullman
1966 "Ambiguity in Context-free Languages", *J. Assoc. Comp. Mach.* 13: 62-88.

Ginzburg, A.
1968 *Algebraic Theory of Automata* (New York: Academic Press).

Gold, E. M.
1967 "Language Identification in the Limit", *Information and Control* 10: 441-74.

Greibach, S. A.
1963 "The Undecidability of the Ambiguity Problem for Minimal Linear Grammars", *Information and Control* 6: 117-25.
1965 "A New Normal Form Theorem for Context-free Phrase Structure Grammars", *J. Ass. Comp. Mach.* 12: 42-52.
1966 "The Unsolvability of the Recognition of Linear Context-free Languages", *J. Ass. Comp. Mach.* 13: 582-87.

Grenander, U.
1967 "Syntax-controlled Probabilities", *Rept. Division Appl. Mathem.* (Brown University, Providence, R.I.).

Hopcroft, J. E., and J. D. Ullman
1969 *Formal Languages and Their Relation to Automata* (Reading, Mass.: Addison-Wesley).

Horning, J. J.
1969 "A Study of Grammatical Inference" (= *Technical Report* CS 139 *Stanford Artificial Intelligence Project*) (Stanford: Computer Science Department).

Huang, T., and K. S. Fu
1971 "On Stochastic Context-free Languages", *Information Sciences* 3: 201-24.

Kleene, S. C.
1952 *Introduction to Metamathematics* (Princeton: Van Nostrand).
1956 "Representation of Events in Nerve Nets and Finite Automata", *Automata Studies*, C. E. Shannon and J. McCarthy (eds.) (Princeton: Princeton University Press).

Knuth, D. E.
1965 "On the Translation of Languages from Left to Right", *Information and Control* 8: 607-39.

Kuroda, S. Y.
1964 "Classes of Languages and Linear-bounded Automata", *Information and Control* 7: 201-23.

Landweber, P. S.
1963 "Three Theorems on Phrase Structure Grammars of Type 1", *Information and Control* 6, 131-36.

McCulloch, W. S., and W. Pitts
1943 "A Logical Calculus of the Ideas Immanent in Nervous Activity", *Bull. Math. Biophysics* 5: 115-33.

Miller, G. A., and N. Chomsky
1957 *Pattern Conception* (Paper for Conference on Pattern Detection, University of Michigan).

Minsky, M. L.
1967 *Computation. Finite and Infinite Machines* (Englewood Cliffs: Prentice-Hall).

Myhill, J.
1960 *Linear Bounded Automata* (= *WADD Technical Note* 60-165) (Wright Air Development Division, Wright-Patterson Air Force Base, Ohio).

Nelson, R. J.
1968 *Introduction to Automata* (New York: Wiley).

Newell, A., J. C. Shaw, and H. A. Simon
1959 "Report on a General Problem-solving Program", *Information Processing, Proc. Intern. Conf. on Information Processing, UNESCO* (Paris, June).

Oettinger, A.
1961 "Automatic Syntactic Analysis and the Pushdown Store", *Structure of Language and its Mathematical Aspects*, R. Jakobson (ed.) (Providence: Amer. Math. Soc.).

Parikh, R. J.
1961 "Language Generating Devices", *Quart. Progr. Rep. MIT Res. Lab. Electr.* 60: 199-212.

Rabin, M. O.
1963 "Probabilistic Automata", *Information and Control* 6: 230-54.

Rabin, M. O., and D. Scott
1959 "Finite Automata and Their Decision Problem", *IBM J. Res.* 3: 115-25.

Salomaa, A.
1969 *Theory of Automata* (Oxford: Pergamon Press).

Solomonoff, R. J.
1958 "The Mechanization of Linguistic Learning", *Proc. Second Intern. Congr. Cybernetics* (Namur), 180-93.
1964a "A Formal Theory of Inductive Reference. Part I", *Information and Control* 7: 1-22.

1964b "A Formal Theory of Inductive Reference. Part II", *Information and Control* 7: 224-54.

Suppes, P.

1970 "Probabilistic Grammars for Natural Languages", *Synthese* 22: 95-116.

Turing, A. M.

1936 "On Computable Numbers, With an Application to the Entscheidungsproblem", *Proc. London Math. Soc.* 42: 230-65.

AUTHOR INDEX

SUBJECT INDEX

(italicized numbers refer to definitions)

Bei Fragen zur Produktsicherheit wenden Sie sich bitte an:
If you have any questions regarding product safety,
please contact:

Walter de Gruyter GmbH
Genthiner Straße 13
10785 Berlin
productsafety@degruyterbrill.com